Once Aboard A
Cornish Lugger

Regards,

Paul Greenw...

Paul Greenwood

ISBN 978-09553648 1 5

Second edition 2011

Published by
Polperro Heritage Press,
Clifton-upon-Teme, Worcestershire WR6 6EN UK
www.polperropress.co.uk

Cover design
Steve Bowgen

Printed by
Berforts Group, Stevenage
Herts.

Contents

I dedicate this book to my old skipper
Thomas Frank 'Moogie' Pengelly
(1920-2002)

Preface

During the last few years of his retirement, I did my very best to persuade my old skipper, Frank Pengelly, that he should put pen to paper and write his life story. If he had done so, it would have been a fascinating and, I think, historically important composition, because he was the very last lugger skipper left in the port of Looe. His knowledge (common to many when he was a young man) had become unique, and he was the final guardian of it. Frank knew the fishing seasons for the drift nets and long lines, as well as the fishing grounds that covered hundreds of square miles of the channel. Without charts he could navigate the coast from Portland Bill to Lands End, his only aids being a clock, a compass and a tide book.

Unfortunately, by the time he did get around to doing something about it, he was very ill and sadly, he passed on before any real progress had been made.

As a boy I served for four and a half years on his lugger the *Iris.* I overcame sea sickness and learned my job on deck working the nets and lines with the other four crew men. Frank, or 'Moogie' as he was known as, always played his cards very close to his chest. He was the skipper, we were the crew, and provided we did our job on deck, that's all he required; there was very little encouragement given to learn more.

There are now only a handful of us left who remember those days, and as 'Moogie' left it too late, I thought that someone ought to try and record the way of life on those boats before it has all faded from living memory.

Frank's knowledge was vast, and I can't pretend for one minute to be able to write the account that he could have written. He was

5

the skipper, I was the boy, so we are coming at the story from two very different angles. But my memories of the time I spent on the *Iris* are still very vivid, (how could they not be?) and by conferring with the few others remaining from those days, I have endeavoured to keep the account as accurate as possible, although by virtue it is a very personal one.

But before I launch into that tale, I should like to paint in the background history of the Cornish lugger. From the mighty three-masted craft of the smuggling and privateering days of the eighteenth century, to the massive fishing fleets of the late nineteenth century, and the twilight years of the mid to late twentieth century. So you will understand that the those few remaining luggers I write about, working out their last days around the Cornish coast in the 1960s were not there by accident, they had a long, and a proud history.

Paul Greenwood
Looe 2007

Introduction

From the seventeenth to the mid twentieth century the lugger, in its various forms, was the principle vessel of the Cornish fishing industry. The early boats were clinker built double-ended craft, between 20 and 40 feet in length, with a wide beam and deep draught. Contemporary drawings show open boats, stepping two and three masts. They were used for hand lining to catch hake, whiting, pollack etc, long lining for turbot, ray and conger as well as working short fleets of hand bred drift nets to catch pilchards, herring and mackerel.

Marketing was limited to what the local fish jowters could hawk around the villages and farms. The only fish handled in bulk were pilchards. These were salt cured and pressed into barrels, to be exported to Spain and Italy as a Lent food and to the West Indies where the plantation owners fed them to their slaves. The early luggers looked to be slow sailers and must have been heavy to row in a calm, but they didn't work very far from home, and as time was not their master, I suppose it mattered little.

Speed only became important when the revenue cutters had to be out paced in the smuggling days of the eighteenth and early nineteenth century. It was then that we caught a glimpse of what the Cornish shipwrights could really do.

The final form of the smuggling lugger was a splendid fully-decked vessel, the largest of them being up to 75 feet in length; both clinker and carvel construction methods were employed. They stepped three masts, allowing a massive press of sail to be set.

It has been recorded that with a 'whole sail' breeze the fastest of them could make the one hundred miles from Cornwall to Roscoff in Brittany in eight hours. That's an average speed of twelve knots, very smart sailing by today's standards let alone two hundred plus years ago.

For their size, these craft were very heavily armed and the greatest of them carried twelve to sixteen cannon on the weather deck, and up to a dozen swivel guns, (these, loaded with grape shot, were the anti personnel weapons of the day) as well as a cutlass and a musket for each member of the crew. When running contraband, 30 men were considered sufficient to work the lugger and her cargo, and if necessary, take on a customs cutter. But when Britain was engaged in one of her many wars against France, Spain, Holland, America etc, letters of marque could be obtained. These documents licensed vessels to go privateering against the enemy. So, as well as running their illicit cargoes, they were also likely to be escorting a valuable prize into harbour. At such times, a crew of up to 60 hands was carried, enough men to fight the ship effectively and put a prize crew aboard the enemy ship, should they carry the day. Looking at the earnings of these vessels, (where records have survived) the money and employment they generated puts them on par with today's tourist industry. Mind you, I suppose there is very little chance of getting killed, imprisoned or hung, for working in a knick-knack shop or a restaurant.

The Cornish smuggling luggers earned for themselves a ferocious reputation, but the crews were well rewarded for the risks they took. For a run to Guernsey or Roscoff and back, a crewman was paid ten pounds, probably more than he would earn in three months working as a fisherman. Any prize money was generously shared, keeping all hands keenly interested in the lugger's success, and at the same time lifting families from poverty to plenty. Meanwhile the venture capitalists reaped huge dividends on their investments, and at the same time kept their hands clean.

Today we can still get some idea of just how big and profitable these contraband operations were because Zephaniah Job, the Polperro 'smuggler's banker' kept detailed accounts of all his transactions, and some of them have survived. For over 20 years Mr Job was agent for, and part investor in, several well-found vessels engaged in smuggling, and if you convert his accounts into today's money the results are quite amazing. He handled some £62 million in transactions of which £37 million was profit to the smugglers, and his was one of two operations active in one small fishing village.

Smuggling was very big business all around the coast of Britain. If ever its true figures could be calculated the results, I am sure, would be truly astounding. These 'Free-traders' as they liked to call themselves, dealt in any imported commodity that the government had seen fit to put a tax on, such as salt, tea, coffee, brandy, silk, wines, perfume and lace. When the French revolution began, a Polperro vessel, then engaged in loading her cargo at Roscoff, rescued some members of the Trelawny family who had been spending the summer at their villa in Brittany. The skipper of the lugger charged these frightened, rather minor Cornish aristocrats more for the Channel crossing than the modern ferry charges today. Spies, criminals, aristocracy on the run - the men with the big fast luggers carried anybody providing they had the gold to pay.

After Napoleon's defeat at Waterloo the government of the day then had an opportunity to do something about the massive loss of revenue it was suffering, and they handed the task over to a well-manned battle-hardened Royal Navy. It proved to be well up to the job, setting up a coastal blockade of the Channel, and it was not long before the risks involved in running contraband became much too high to remain profitable. The big luggers (those that hadn't been captured) were disarmed and re-employed as humble coastal traders. Smuggling did continue, but of necessity it became a low profile, small time operation. The glory days were now over.

The fishing lugger meanwhile had remained a slow cumbersome affair. Speed costs money and if it is not essential, then no one will invest in it.

In 1859 the great engineer I.K. Brunel completed his railway bridge over the river Tamar, and that changed everything. Cornwall was now no longer a remote, virtually inaccessible county. Fresh fish (amongst many other commodities) could now be transported to the markets of London, Manchester and Birmingham, and to make the best of these new opportunities, larger, faster and better-designed boats were required. These new craft had to be able to work fishing grounds a long way from their home port, and then return swiftly to land their catches, fresh and in time for the market trains. Prime fish, boxed and well iced for the journey, made top prices on the city markets.

Once again the shipwrights had to come up with the answers. Their forefathers had excelled in the quest for speed in the smuggling days, and now these men had to rise to the challenge of the opportunities being offered by the railways.

But the new class of lugger didn't appear overnight from the drawing board of some genius naval architect. No, the final form of the Cornish lugger evolved steadily over a couple of generations, the fruit of observation, new ideas and experience. A skipper wanting a boat built would discuss with the boat builder of his choice, the sort of craft he had in mind, her length, beam, draught, shape of transom etc. Bearing these instructions in mind, the builder would take a piece of clear pine and carve to scale a half model, then present it to the skipper for final adjustments. Paring a bit off here and there, they would eventually arrive at the final shape of the new boat. This model would then be sawn down at the datum lines, the resulting sections provided the shapes for the frames of the full sized craft.

A more primitive method used was to build the boat entirely by eye. The shipwright would lay down the keel, put up the stem post, sternpost, deadwoods and transom. Next, three frames would be made and mounted on the keel, battens would then be nailed around fore and aft to give the general shape of the hull. The skipper and the builder would then spend time eyeing things up, fairing the frames in here and there until they got her looking right; 'suant' was the word used to describe it. When both parties were satisfied with their efforts, the build could proceed. This method of construction worked, but a boat could well end up being faster on one tack than the other, for the simple reason that her hull could be very different in shape from port to starboard.

Another peculiarity of some of the Cornish boats was that, when afloat, their stem and frames appeared to be slanting backwards. This was because in the building, everything had been set up perpendicular from the keel, and of course when the boat was afloat she drew around six feet aft and three feet forward, throwing the keel at least eighteen inches out of level, it was a curious effect. Most shipwrights would set everything up from the waterline so as all looked fair when she was afloat, but some of the old men never altered their ways and boats were built with backward raking stems right up to the 1930s.

There were no minimum standards laid down for boat construction. The amount and quality of timber in a hull would vary, governed by the money available to the man having it built. A large budget could mean heavy oak frames set at 16 inch centres, sheathed with pitch pine planking maybe two inches thick. A tight budget could mean that the oak frames were much lighter and set out at twenty inch centres, sheathed with one and a quarter inch red pine planking. But, as Looe shipwright Arthur Collins used to say, "It's not the weight of wood in a boat, it's the way it's fitted," and the Cornish shipwrights could certainly 'fit wood'. Hull planks were cut to such a degree of accuracy that caulking was unnecessary, plank edges were bevelled to fit together perfectly, resulting in even the most meanly built of luggers being well up to the work required of them. And much was required of them, in the days of large families and no social services, where people lived and died by the results of their own efforts. One lugger with a crew of six men could well be responsible for feeding and clothing as many as 40 people. From babes in arms, to dependants too old or too ill to work any more, a heavy burden indeed for the men at sea.

The Cornish lugger was unique and could not be mistaken for any other class of vessel around the British Isles, except for maybe the Manx 'Nicky', but they were based on the Cornish lugger to begin with. Every boat yard had its own 'signature', and every skipper had his own ideas of how his boat should look. Fleets of them were built, (well over a hundred worked from Looe over the years) you could see their pedigree, they were alike, but no two were ever the same. The majority, for all their individuality, were just good working craft providing a frugal living for her people. But there were exceptions at either end of the scale; the odd one would turn out to be a complete 'dog', a slow sailer and an indifferent sea boat, giving everyone aboard a hard time for as long as she was worked. The Looe boats *Dove* and the *Harvest Home* (FY 159), were two such examples.

Equally rare were the luggers whose speed and sweetness of line made them the talk of the coast; in a county famed for such craft they had to be something very special to stand out. The *Talisman* (FY 242) of Looe and the *Sunshine* (FY 222) of Mevagissey were probably two of the finest examples.

This new breed of lugger was between 36 and 45 feet in length, with a beam of twelve to fourteen feet, drawing six to seven feet of water. With a straight stem and a long sleek bow for going to weather, they had neat sterns for running, and a graceful shear line to show off their good looks. They were two-masted, setting a huge dipping lug main sail on the fore mast, and a standing lug sail on the mizzen; a mizzen staysail and jib could be set in light airs or when on a long passage.

These boats could carry their nets and lines plus a big catch of fish in all weathers, while remaining safe and stable. By the 1890s they had reached their extreme form. In the quest for speed they had gone as far as possible without jeopardising their seaworthiness, and by now even the finest gentlemen's yachts of the day had a job to match the best of them.

For their grace and beauty, the Breton fishermen called them the 'swallows of the sea', and by now fully-decked, the final form of the Cornish lugger had evolved. The fish were plentiful and trade was brisk, railway transport and fine new boats had opened up the Cornish fishermen's horizons. As well as working the home pilchard and herring season, they fished for mackerel with their drift nets off the south west coast of Ireland, while some worked long lines for ray, conger and turbot out as far as the coast of Brittany.

Others followed the herring shoals along the west coast of Scotland and on up to the Shetland Isles and then down into the north sea ending the season at Scarborough on the Yorkshire coast.

It was while returning to her home port of St Ives from the herring fishery at Scarborough in 1902, that the *Lloyd* SS 5 made the six hundred mile voyage in just 50 hours, an average speed of twelve knots. To drive a boat that hard, her skipper must have had nerves of iron. Many of the luggers had made the trip in 70 hours, still a very respectable eight knots average. But the record for long distance voyaging must surely rest with skipper Joseph Nicholls and his crew who, in 1846, sailed the 38 foot lugger *Mystery* from Newlyn to Australia in 116 days. This was several years before the modern design came in, and the *Mystery* would have probably been an open boat in the amidships working area and of the old fashioned cod's-head mackerel's-tail hull form.

By the late 1880s the fishing industry had reached its zenith. 570 first class luggers were registered in the ports and harbours of Cornwall employing 3,500 men and boys at sea, and probably double that number in ancillary trades ashore. Although their numbers declined continually from here onwards, it would be another 108 years before the last working lugger landed her final catch.

Just before the 1914-18 war small petrol-paraffin engines became available, enabling the boats to leave and enter harbour more easily, and make headway in a calm. An old fisherman told me that when the engines were first introduced they thought they were in heaven as their lives were made so much easier; another bonus was the boats began to last longer. I reckoned the obvious reason for that was oil and paraffin leaking from the engines and soaking into the timber had a preserving effect, but he reckoned it killed off most of the 'sow-pigs'(woodlice) that lived in droves on a wooden vessel, weakening them over the years by eating them from the inside out. I really don't know what to make of that yarn, but he was there so there must be something in it.

The *Undaunted* (FY 393) of Looe, owned by brothers Ness and Johnny Richards was one of the first luggers to have an engine installed. They used to charge 6d a boat to tow the others in or out of the harbour to save the crew having to row or pay a shore gang to pull them to the pier head. Evidently at slack water she could tow as many as six boats at a time, all that with a seven HP engine. I think the horses in those engines must have been a lot bigger than they are today.

Those early engines required a fair bit of maintenance to keep them in good running order. The cylinder heads would have to be taken off at regular intervals for a de-coke and for the valves to be ground in. The magneto and spark plugs had to be cleaned and set up with the right gaps, and once a year or so, the big end bearing caps had to be filed down to take the slack out of them. One man on each boat, known as the 'Engine Driver', would be responsible for this work as well as their operation at sea.

These engines had a dual horse-power rating, i.e. 6/7 or 12/14 etc. This was because they ran on two different fuels, petrol and paraffin. Each engine had two tanks, a small tank for petrol and a larger one for paraffin, the pipes from each connected to a two-way tap on the carburettor. To start up, the tap was turned to petrol and the carb flooded, then the choke was applied and the magneto was retarded (this was to stop the engine backfiring and injuring the man cranking the handle). Upon starting, as the engine warmed up, the choke was taken off, and the magneto advanced, it would now be running at the top HP rating. When the engine was judged to be hot enough, the fuel was turned over to the much cheaper paraffin, but the HP dropped to the lower rating.

Initially the engines had no gearboxes or any form of clutch, meaning no neutral and no astern. The shaft was coupled directly to the crankshaft, so that when the engine was started you were away. Therefore, to have any sort of control when entering harbour, the length of time a carburettor full of fuel lasted had to be known to within a few seconds. At the critical moment the fuel would be cut off and if all went well the engine stopped, leaving the boat with just enough 'way' to come along side the quay in a dignified and safe manner, with maybe just a bit of drudging here and there. But if things went wrong, and there was nobody on the quay to catch a rope, then the bow had to be run in between the sterns of the next two boats moored ahead, or scraped up the quay until she stopped. You can just imagine the shouting and swearing, crashing and scrunching that must have gone on at times in the early days of engines.

Thankfully, gearboxes were very soon introduced, giving the boats neutral and a brake in the form of being able to go astern. But the early boxes with their cone clutches were liable to jam in gear, so the 'Engine Driver' always had a lump of ballast iron handy to belt the lever with, should that happen. As problematical as those early engines were, nobody wanted to go back to sails and oars. Through the 1920s and 1930s engines steadily advanced in both power and design. There were many different makes and horse powers to choose from, but by far the most popular with the fishermen were those made at the Kelvin engineering works in Glasgow. By the mid 1930s the ideal power combination for a lugger proved to be the four cylinder 30 HP, with a straight drive gearbox for the main engine and a 13 HP driving through a two to one reduction gearbox for a wing engine. The maximum hull speed of eight knots could be obtained when the two engines were driving together, and the wing motor on its own was powerful enough to work the boat up to the nets and lines in all but the worst of weather, as well as being very economical on fuel.

These motors were very far from maintenance free, and their performance certainly reflected the amount of TLC they received. But most of the engine drivers on the boats took great pride in looking after their charges, and were genuinely sorry to see them craned out in the late 1940s and early 1950s to be replaced by the more advanced, and efficient diesel engines.

Upon the outbreak of the First World War, the backbone of the fishing fleet (all the young fit men and the best of the boats) was called up for service in the Royal and Merchant navies, leaving only the old men and boys to carry on as best they could, working their nets and lines close in, up and down the coast, for fear of U Boats etc. Then with the coming of peace in 1919, the men who had survived those hellish years returned home, and later the boats that had been requisitioned (those that had survived ordeal by matlo) were released by the Admiralty.

When the fishing fleet refitted and got back to sea, what a surprise the men had. The deep fishing grounds had lain virtually undisturbed for five years, and were now teeming with fish. When they shot the long lines, every hook came up with a prime fish on it. When working the drift nets, the resulting pilchard catches loaded the smaller boats down to danger point. Nobody had experienced anything like it. What's more, a hungry post war Europe needed feeding, so the huge catches that were being landed had a ready market and made good money.

Here then was another massive boom in the fishing industry. The best of the existing fleet was modernised with new and more powerful engines, while the smaller older craft were sold off and replaced by a new design of motor lugger then entering service. These boats carried their beam well forward and were bigger in the bilge than the old sailing luggers. At that time they could also boast two and sometimes three petrol/paraffin engines pushing out as much as 30 HP.

Sails were reduced to a small standing lug mizzen and a leg of mutton foresail, known as a 'marmaduke'. This was enough canvas to stop her rolling when making a passage out and back to the lining grounds, or to help her along should an engine refuse duty. Wheelhouses were now being fitted, doing away with tiller steering. They were bolted to the deck just forward of the mizzen mast, a wheel and gypsy operated chains back to a quadrant on the rudder. Just big enough for one man to stand up in, they were a godsend in reducing hypothermia and exposure in wintertime. All this modernisation made life at sea a lot more bearable and, because of this, the men started to last a lot longer. In the sailing days most were ashore, worn out by their mid-forties through gruelling hard work, exposure and poor nutrition, having started their sea going career at eleven or twelve years of age. But now, although many were still starting at a very tender age, they found they were able to carry on working into their fifties and sixties.

Much longer fleets of drift nets could be worked, as the boats no longer had to be hauled to their gear with a hand operated foot line capstan. With the introduction of the motor powered line hauler or 'jinny' in the 1920s, it became possible to work 6,000 hooks of long line on a tide, as against 4,000 with a man powered hauler or 2,000 when hauled by hand.

Meanwhile the fish stayed plentiful, market prices were holding up and catch records were being broken. During the herring season of 1920, for example, a Looe lugger, the *May Blossom* (FY 51) shot her nets in Bigbury Bay. She was the only boat out that night because a south-west gale looked to be brewing up, sending the rest of the fleet back into harbour. The skipper, Roger Dingle, and his crew were all young married men with families to support, so it took an awful lot of bad weather to make them turn and run for home. They rode to the nets for just long enough to have their supper then, with the engines cranked into life, all hands donned their oilskins and sea boots ready to begin the night's work. By this time, the rising gale was starting to make life very uncomfortable, with an ugly breaking sea and driving rain. Roger and his crew were in for a hard night. Nevertheless, after several gruelling hours of work, they prevailed and the nets were once more stowed back into the net room, and a huge catch of herring was their reward. The *May Blossom* was now deeply laden, her fish room was full and she was loaded rail to rail on deck. The weather was much too bad to try and get back to land at the fish market on Plymouth Barbican; their only option was to run before the gale and land their catch at Brixham. So, with both engines at full throttle, the mizzen was sheeted away and the foresail hoisted to give her all the help they could. The fate of the *May Blossom* and her crew was now in the lap of the gods; all they could do was to hang on tight and keep pumping.

They shot around Bolt Head, the skipper edging her out to gain a good berth off Prawl Point. The wind was blowing like 'Barney's Bull' and the seas were big and breaking. Several stone of fish was washed over the side, but very little could be done about that.

In a welter of breaking seas they battled around Start Point and then, giving the Skerries bank a wide berth, the course was altered to the north east, right before the wind. Now running bends deep in foam, they surfed up to Berry Head and the welcoming haven of Tor Bay. You can just imagine the jaw-dropping disbelief of those around Brixham harbour that morning as this heavily laden lugger and her weary crew tied up along side the quay to land their catch. They had been the only boat out on the entire coast that night, and the fish merchants were desperate for herring. How many cran of fish they landed has not been recorded, but the amount it made has: the catch sold for £634, not a bad day's work nowadays, but in 1920 it was a fortune. They arrived back in Looe to a heroes' welcome, and the *May Blossom*'s owner, Dick 'Clubs' Pengelly, had a gilded cockerel carved and mounted at the masthead, denoting that she was cock of the fleet.

Back then, 30 shillings to two pounds was a week's wage for a working man. Roger Dingle's daughter, Gwen, remembered her father bringing home his wages: for that one night's work he had earned £90, and with this, his wife bought the family a cottage. To earn a whole year's wages in one night, and that enough to buy a home with, the *May Blossom*'s catch can surly have had few equals for its purchasing power.

The Cornish fishing industry was enjoying prosperous times and for some, as in the case of the *May Blossom*, it was exceptional, but it was not to last. The slump of the late 1920s ushered in hard times with a vengeance, boat owners went into debt while their crews were unable to pay the rent on their cottages or the grocery bills at the end of the week. Many well found luggers were sold off to the highest bidder, while the men who had crewed on them were glad to take jobs labouring on the roads, or any employment at all that would feed the family and pay the rent. Those who couldn't find a job had to live hand to mouth, and hunger was not unknown.

When a vessel was sold, the former owner was then able pay his outstanding debts and maybe put a little money in the bank. But it was the jobless crewman and his family who really started to suffer. Hard times forced Ned Ham, a Looe skipper, to sell his boat the *Adela* (FY 169). Later on when he saw the hardships his old crew and their families were going through he tried to buy her back from the new owner, so that he could re-employ them and try to make them some sort of a living. As poor as it might have been, it would still have been much better than nothing at all. But it was no deal; the new owner would not budge. This played on poor Ned's mind so badly that he eventually committed suicide in the front room of his home at 'Port Cottage' up West Looe Hill, by drowning himself in a bucket of water.

Another former owner tried to drown himself for similar reasons, and if it hadn't been so very sad, it would have been farcical. He made his attempt at oblivion by tying one end of a length of rope to a 56lbs weight and the other end around his neck, then jumped into the river. Fortunately, the rope was too long and so, firmly anchored, he swam around in circles until he was rescued.

Towards the end of the 1920s things did level out a bit, fish prices were very poor, but there was plenty of fish to be caught, so a week's wages could be scraped up if you worked hard enough. Many of the younger fishermen spent the summers crewing on the J class yachts that attended the big regattas of the day, racing in the Solent, Torbay and the Clyde. Others worked on yachts doing a summer season in the Mediterranean where the wages were poor but they lived 'all found' and were likely to receive a small retainer in the winter. Yet another way a fisherman could boost a meagre and uncertain income was to join the Royal Naval Reserve. A small yearly retainer was paid, and in return, the men had to attend an annual two-week's training on a ship or naval shore establishment, for which they received a naval rating's pay. In fact, most of the men classed that fortnight as their annual holiday.

The 1930s were also very depressing times for the fishermen, but always the hope was that things just had to improve, though unfortunately they didn't. The year 1937 must surely go down as one of the bleakest in the history of the Cornish fishing industry. In that year, the government of the day put an embargo on exports to Italy in retaliation for Mussolini's invasion of Abyssinia. This caused the pilchard trade to all but collapse, because the vast bulk of the Cornish salters' produce was exported to that country to be eaten as a lent food. There is an old rhyme concerning that trade.

18

Here's a health to the Pope and may he relent
And extend by six months the terms of his lent
For 'tis very well known between the two poles
There is nothing like pilchards for the saving of souls

The embargo was an unmitigated disaster. What effect it had on the Italian people, I don't know, but it certainly punished a lot of people in Cornwall.

The next body blow to the fishing industry in that dreadful year was the complete failure of the herring fishery. Every October shoals of herring used to appear off the south-west coast to spawn in the big sandy bays. Fleets of drifters from all the major fishing ports of Britain would arrive to partake of this harvest. In 1937 the boats appeared, but the expected fish failed to show up. In the previous year's herring season, a number of trawlers had been active in the spawning bays, trying to catch herring in their trawls. They enjoyed a certain amount of success, but every haul they made not only filled their decks with herring, but with spawn as well. The fish they caught were boxed up and stowed down below while the spawn, now dead, was shovelled back over the side, and around the bay they went again to repeat the process.

When, there were no herring to be caught the following year by trawlers or drifters, nobody could believe it. Their absence was put down to their just being late, and the boats burnt hundreds of gallons of fuel between them, hunting for shoals that would never arrive for the simple reason that they no longer existed. In the end, the chandlers stopped crediting the boats with fuel that they were pretty sure they weren't going to get paid for, and that was that. The drifters returned to their home ports, the crews were skint and the skippers were in debt.

The Cornish fishing industry had been on a knife-edge for years, but the twin disasters of 1937 really put the skids under it. From then on, the fleet shrank rapidly as boats were sold off for whatever money could be raised on them. The only ones to survive were the most-hard working and frugal of skippers who hung on to their boats, grimly hoping for better times.

With the outbreak of the Second World War, as in the First, every fit and able-bodied man was called up for service in the navy. The best of the boats were also requisitioned for war work, leaving yet again a few old men and boys to carry on as they might. Those who did fish through the war years made a very good living, although the grounds they were able to work were very limited. The country needed all the food it could get, so the government now controlled the fish prices, which meant the men knew exactly what they would be paid per stone for each species of fish and if they all had good catches the price didn't plunge to the floor as always happened on the auction market. Fishing in peacetime is a hard and dangerous occupation, but in wartime the dangers were trebled. Not only did they risk an encounter with the enemy in the form of E-boats, submarines and aircraft, but at night the boats were forbidden to show any lights. This of course greatly increased the risk of collision. Add to that a total black-out ashore, and the wartime fishing skipper was facing some fairly daunting problems. As protection for the Looe fleet, the lugger *Our Boys* had a heavy machine gun mounted on her foredeck. Fortunately they never had to use it in anger, but once a week they opened up with it for practice: "Shooting at the shags," Bill Pye, her skipper, used to say. Two Mevagissey boats, the *Ibis* and the *Pride of the West* were machine-gunned by a German fighter plane but, as luck would have it, he missed both of them. A Plymouth boat was not so lucky however; she was machine-gunned and sunk with all hands while fishing beyond the Eddystone lighthouse.

When peace was declared, and the men were demobbed from the forces, they returned home to exactly the same situation their fathers and elder brothers had experienced when they returned home from WW1. The fishing grounds had had five years' rest, the fish were plentiful, and a starving Europe needed all the food it could get.

The luggers (now numbering about 40 in Cornwall) were made ready for sea, along with their drift nets and long lines. The first boats away returned home with catches the like of which most fishermen only dream of. Fish were teaming, to the extent that some boats had their long lines rendered useless because they were coming up with a mature fish on every hook, and as they circled around the line between the seabed and the surface, the rope backing would become completely unlaid.

Fleets of driftnets were lost through the sheer weight of

pilchards taking them to the bottom. Such happenings were now more an inconvenience than a disaster. The fishermen were once more riding the crest of a wave. The county's pilchard works or 'salters' were exporting to Italy again, and six canneries had opened up, tinning pilchards in tomato sauce or olive oil for the home and export markets. During the long line or 'boulter' season, the railways transported many thousands of stone of prime turbot, ray and conger etc, to the fish markets of the major cities.

The boatyards were also very busy as orders came in for new boats, taking out the old petrol/paraffin engines and installing new diesel engines in the existing fleet. These were the first true marine engine, unaffected by damp, virtually maintenance free and running on a very cheap fuel.

A few new motor luggers were built to bolster the ageing fleet, but more favoured for new build especially at Looe, were the smaller, cheaper general-purpose boats now coming off the designers drawing board. Their origins could not be mistaken, a straight stem with a neat transom and sweet sheer line. They were the luggers' younger sisters.

Thirty to 38 feet in length, nine to twelve feet in the beam and drawing four to five feet of water, they were high in the hull as they had no bulwarks; a long foredeck accommodated the engines and cabin, a full width open backed wheelhouse came next and a small tight deck aft covered the steering gear. The main working area amidships was covered with a hatch board deck about waist height down from the rail. They were known as 'quatters' because they weren't considered big enough to work the offshore grounds, but instead earned their living on the home grounds, or the 'quatt'. Four men could make a living drifting and long-lining; two men could work her crabbing, or one man could take day-trippers angling in the summer months. A very handy craft indeed. Fine examples of that class were the *Claire*, skipper Charlie Butters; the *Silver Spray*, skipper Edgar Williams; the *Endeavour*, skipper Fernley Soady, and the *Paula*, skipper Bill Butters.

But the lugger was still the mainstay of the Cornish fishing fleet, be she newly launched or a craft that had first seen service in the middle years of Queen Victoria's reign. The skippers themselves were exceptional men. They would have probably served a minimum of ten years working under their father or uncle, the then skipper, learning every aspect of seamanship, knowledge of the fishing grounds and developing the steady nerve and great strength of character needed to wrest a living for five men and their families from the sea. In the days before radio you couldn't shout for help if things went wrong, caught in a gale, long lining 60 miles off shore. The skipper's responsibilities must have weighed very heavily at times.

In the long lining season there were many different areas of ground to be worked, with names like 'Klondike', 'Ray Pits' and 'Stone Light Dipping'. The skippers knew how the tide flowed over them at ebb and flood, and the fish to be caught on them: sand and gravel for ray and turbot, rock and rough ground for conger, ling and pollack.

When working the drift nets, they knew where to expect the pilchard shoals and at what time of year. An old saying goes: 'When the corn is in the shock, then the pilchards go to rock' meaning that around harvest time the shoals are to be found close in shore. Another says that pilchards were 'Food, money and light, all in one night', the light referring to the days when pilchard oil (a bi-product of the salt curing process) was burnt in the lamps. Their knowledge was vast, and very much more than could be accumulated in one lifetime. It was the result of many lifetimes' experience passed on down through the generations, and added to by each skipper. Charts were never used; each skipper carried his own chart in his head and could navigate, fair weather or foul, day or night around large areas of the coast. Unfortunately none of this knowledge was ever written down; the location of the grounds and when to fish them, the compass courses and estimated times to get to them were all committed to memory, and are now lost.

Their methods of fishing were ecologically sound. Drift nets would catch plenty of fish, but never decimate the shoals. Long lines did no damage to the grounds they were shot on, and only caught mature fish. Every generation left plenty of good fishing for the next, and very little (if any) harm was done to the balance of nature. But by the middle of the twentieth century, technology and progress became the watchwords. Why catch part of a shoal of fish when the whole shoal can be caught with a purse seine or ring net? Why try to tempt a few mature fish to take the baited hooks of a long line when, with a modern trawler, you can go on the offensive and catch them hungry or not?

The luggers of Cornwall were considered to be retrogressive, their methods of fishing had hardly changed in centuries and, in truth, it was only the boom after the two world wars that had seen them continue thus far. So, while the Cornish boats were enjoying the good times, progress and politics were lining up yet again to deal them a blow. During the war Belgium, Holland and France had lost nearly all of their fishing fleets and, as they needed food as much as we did, their governments were heavily subsidising the design and construction of fleets of modern trawlers.

These new vessels soon started to become a real headache to anyone working long lines, to the extent that the luggers had nearly as much chance of having their gear towed away, as coming home with a catch of fish. Over a period of time, the trawlers have reduced the old lining grounds to near deserts. Any mature fish on them now must be suffering from acute loneliness.

Yet another blow was dealt to the industry by our own government when, in 1955, a trade agreement was drawn up with South Africa. A small part of the deal saw Britain importing South African tinned pilchards, retailing on the home market at 2d a tin cheaper than the Cornish product. It wasn't long before the canneries started to feel the pinch and, in a bid to compete, they dropped the price paid to the boats for pilchards from 4/6d (22p) to 3/6d (17p) per stone. However, it did not help. They began to lose orders from the retailers and, one by one, they closed down. The salters were also losing orders. Tastes were changing on the continent, and a new generation of consumers was not as fond of salt fish as their parents and grandparents had been. To crown it all, the pilchard shoals changed their habits for some reason, and were no longer to be found off the Cornish coast during the winter months. Now there was nothing to be earned with either nets or lines, from the end of November to March.

Deathblows were raining down on an industry that had sustained itself for centuries, making it only a matter of a few short years before it would be consigned to history. By 1960 many of the once-thriving, bustling harbours of Cornwall echoed more to the ghosts of the past than to the activities of the living. Looe was a typical example. Quayside warehouses stood empty and locked up, the fish market had closed down, fishermen's stores and net-lofts were being turned into cafes or workshops. The few remaining boats seemed to huddle up together for comfort, leaving whole areas of the quayside empty and deserted.

For a few brief weeks each summer the port would come back to life, but the voices to be heard echoed of accents well north of the Tamar. These were holidaymakers going out for a day's angling, or on trips around the bay, and thank goodness they did because for several years it was really only their custom that kept the whole harbour from penury.

The Looe fleet by now consisted of about 15 quatters fitted out with seats and fishing rods for the holiday trade. Most of these boats lay idle from October to May. Two or three of them might take aboard a fleet of nets and have a go for the pilchards in early spring or autumn, crewed by skippers of the other laid-up boats; a couple more worked a few crab pots. Only two boats now worked through the winter months: the two quatters, the *Renee* (skipper Leonard Pengelly) and the *Ella* (skipper Billy Hocking). These two went trawling, and their catches were driven to Plymouth market each morning.

In its hey-day, Looe had boasted a fleet of 60 luggers: by the early 1960s only five remained. They were the *Our Boys* (FY 221) built in 1904, skipper Bill Pengelly; the *Our Daddy* (FY 7), launched 1920, skipper A.J. Pengelly; the *Iris* (FY 357) launched 1921, skipper Frank Pengelly; the *Guide Me* (FY 233), built 1911, skipper Ned Pengelly; and the *Eileen* (FY 310), built 1920, skipper Ernie Toms. Two others had survived until 1960 but had been sold off due to the crews retiring and no young men coming into the fishing business to take their place. They were the *John Wesley* (FY 35) taken to Falmouth to be used as a house boat, later to be refitted and put back to sea for another twenty years when the mackerel fishery began, and the *Our Girls* (FY 54), sister ship to the *Our Boys* (FY 221). She went to Portsmouth to be converted to a motor yacht.

The three constructed in the post WW1 boom replaced (in order,) the *Sweet Home* (FY 221), *Olive* (FY 108), and the *Little Charlie* (FY52), three swift little sailing luggers of the 1890s. The *Little Charlie*, skipper 'Watt' Toms, had been a real flyer and used to win a lot of silverware at the local regattas; in fact, after one exciting dual someone composed a rhyme to commemorate it that went.

Old Peter Ferris
He lived up Beech Terrace
He built the Little Charlie
A boat of no size
That went to Mevagissey
And won the first prize.

That was back in the glory days, now long past. A new fishery, bringing all the ports around the coast of Cornwall back to life once more, was just over the horizon, but it would have nothing to do with drift nets or long lines. That ancient fishery was breathing its last in Cornwall.

Those four years that I worked with Moogie set me up well for the rest of my sea-going career, because nothing subsequently ever seemed as hard or as physically demanding as the time I spent working on the deck of the *Iris*. As fondly as I look back and write about those years, believe you me, I would not want to do it again.

1

Early Days

I was 16-years-old and brimming with youthful certainty and optimism. I had just won a three-month battle with my parents to gain their permission to go fishing. Not angling with a rod and line for a hobby or sport, but to join the lugger *Iris* as one of her crew.

As a child I had always played around on the water, out with Dad in his dinghy sailing around Talland Bay, towing rubber eels to catch pollack; expeditions to Looe or Polperro on fine summer afternoons, or rowing into all the little gullies and beaches gathering driftwood for a barbeque.

When I was thirteen I bought a boat of my own. She cost me the princely sum of one pound: a poor worn-out old thing that had lain for years upside down in the withy bed above Talland beach. She was in a dreadful condition and, in truth, her next role should really have been to star at a Guy Fawkes party, not go back in the water. The keel was badly hogged and, having been upside down for so long, the bottom of her sagged in sympathy. In an attempt to cure this, some friends and I draped her over an upended 45 gallon drum. This treatment got rid of the hogging temporarily and, hoping to make her stay that way, we nailed a stout piece of driftwood along the length of the keel. The bottom, both inside and out, was then liberally coated with a mixture of beach tar and cement dust, brushed on smoking hot from an oil drum over a bonfire. Tide line enamel (paint tins washed up on the beach, their contents scraped into one can and all stirred up together with paraffin) was used to paint up the rest of her, finishing up a delicate shade of mauve/brown. She was 14 feet long, clinker built and of an unknown vintage. When out in her we had to bail continually, and the bottom actually undulated when going over a wave. But she was all mine, and with a gang of friends we had endless fun in her. Sails would be rigged and we would skid off to lee, eventually having to row and bail for ages to get back to the beach again.

After a south-westerly gale, a big ground sea would be breaking on the sand bar at low tide and that was when we would go surfing, not with boards, but in the boat. Six hands were needed for this sport, one on each of the four oars, one forward to keep the bows down and bail with a bucket, and myself aft, one hand on the steering oar, the other bailing with another bucket. One thing you didn't need for this sport was any imagination. How we didn't drown, I don't know.

The boat was dragged out into waist-deep water and the person at the bow would hang on while the rest of us scrambled aboard and made ready at the oars; the bow man then hopped in and we would start pulling through the breakers. Trying to hold her steady while riding over a cresting sea, the bow pointing at the sky, the boat seeming to hover balanced on her transom. Sliding down into a trough the other side, the next wave might be breaking, burying us over our heads in white sun-filled foam. Many is the time we were tipped end for end or totally swamped, boat and crew being washed back onto the sand in one big heap. There, laughing at the mishap and wiping the salt water from our eyes and hair, we would gather up the oars and buckets, tip the water out of the boat and launch out again. Given half a chance though, we would make it to the back of the breakers, bucket out half the ocean, then hold station facing the beach, awaiting that big wave. Along it would come, cresting feet above the rest, and half a dozen good strokes on the oars would see us catch the wave as it broke. Oars were then boated and, with myself on the steering oar desperately trying to keep her straight, we would hurtle towards the beach in a mass of spume to be (if all went to plan) left high, but far from dry, on the sand as the wave retreated. Sometimes we would end up skidding down the face of a wave, totally out of control and at a most perilous angle. If we didn't get swamped we would be driven onto the rocks that flanked the sand bar, crashing to halt, then to drag her off and up the beach to inspect for damage. Occasionally a plank would be stove in, but a strip of hardboard generously buttered with tar and nailed over the damage soon had us away again.

Another memory that stands out is of going wrecking after a south-west gale. A friend of mine, Kevin Curtis, rang up one morning to say a yacht had been wrecked during the night under the cliffs at Polperro. As the storm baulks were down, no one in the village could get out and there were loads of stuff for the taking, just washing in the tide line. The gale of the previous night had died down, leaving just a big ground swell. Launching off Talland beach, the boat rode the seas like a little duck as the two of us pulled towards the cliffs where the wreck had struck.

Backing in on the swell, we loaded up with all sorts of treasures: a bottle of gas and a can of petrol, lengths of rope, bits of wood, a rug and loads of other things that we grabbed just because they were there. Being first on the scene, our greed was well up so we decided to row over to a cove where the tide seemed to be taking much of the wreckage. At the mouth of the cove we held station, bow to sea, to work out how we might make a landing. We made a landing alright - a great wave came cresting in and tipped the boat bow over stern, washing us all of a heap right up to the head of the cove. Luckily the boat jammed behind a rock and Kevin and I held on to it, as the backwash of the sea scoured the cove clean of everything, including my bottom boards and paddles. The wreckers had become the wrecked; Neptune was obviously not happy with our avarice and had decided to chamfer a bit off our egos. It was Easter time, the air was cold, the sea was colder, and we stood there like a pair of drowned shags, with nothing but an empty boat and lucky to have that.

After dragging the poor old boat up clear of the tide line, Kevin and I then had to scramble up the cliff through the gorse and marram grass to reach the cliff path. There we went our separate ways home, soggy and crestfallen. A couple of days later, when the ground sea had gone down, I returned in another boat to tow mine back to Talland. The wrecked yacht was Norwegian, being sailed back single-handed from the Mediterranean; the skipper's body was washed up some days later and I was told that his watch was still working.

Playing around in boats as a schoolboy led to more adventures, in the form of night trips out pilchard drifting from Polperro on Jack Joliffe's little lugger, the *One Accord* (FY185). This was great fun, working the dip net, pumping out, and helping to land the catch at the end of the night. Mind you, as I soon found out, this was a very soft introduction to the real thing, going out when the fancy took you, and then only if the weather was fine. Even then I used occasionally to get seasick, and my bedroom would be all a-sway when back home the next morning.

The *One Accord* was about 38 feet long and had originally been an open-decked St Ives gig. Jack had bought her when he was demobbed from the navy after the war, refitting her with decks, bulwarks and new engines plus a little one-man wheelhouse. The four-man crew had sailed together for many years: Tom Joliffe, a tall wry sort of fellow who always did the steering; Arkie Pucky drove the engines; Edmund Curtis was chief net mender, while Jacko the skipper kept an overall eye on things and smoked his pipe.

Because the *One Accord* was the only remaining pilchard drifter working from Polperro, she had to land her catches in Looe and then steam back to her home port, a distance of about three miles. On more than one occasion, when the sea was glassy calm, Jack would drop me off in Talland Bay to save me the walk home from Polperro. They would be those rare occasions when he actually took charge of his own boat. Nudging her gently into a gully on the west side of the bay under what was known as 'Dickey Bunt's' house, Arkie would be up in the bows looking down into the water: "Rock here, just to port of us, Jack!" he would shout. "Another one ahead of us, and it's not very deep." The skipper would be calmly drawing on his pipe and taking very little notice of Arkie's rock warnings. Giving a touch here and there on the wheel and a nudge on the engine, he would have her along side in the gully. I would await his order before leaping onto the rocks, then turn around to wave goodbye and thank him as they went astern back out into the bay. Scrambling up the cliff to join the path, I was soon home in bed. The first time Jack put me ashore in that gully, Tommy Toms who was out in his crabber, the *Sheila*, hauling pots, looked up from his labours and, for a moment, was convinced that Tom had nodded off at the wheel and had put the *One Accord* ashore.

Mind you, Jacko wasn't averse to scraping the odd rock. The word in Polperro was that if you wanted to know where the rocks were up and down the shore, ask Jack: he had been up on every one of them.

On another occasion, when battling back from Looe to Polperro in heavy rain and a rising south-west gale, I was sent down into the cabin for safety. Sitting below in such conditions it wasn't long before I was sick all over the cabin sole. For a while I pondered how I was going to explain the mess when we got to the moorings, but I had no need to worry. The old *One Accord* worked a fair bit in poor weather, so it wasn't long before the bilge water was lapping over the cabin sole, washing away all the evidence of my mishap. But seasickness aside, what a wonderful sensation it was to go from all the bang crash wallop and flying spray of a rising gale to escape into the tranquillity and safety of Polperro harbour. Soon we were riding snug on the mooring chains, but it was quite a while before we could scull ashore in the punt and go home. Arkie reckoned we had at least half the Channel to pump out of her.

Looking back now, I can't really say why I decided to go fishing for a living. Maybe it was the freedom and independence that it seemed to offer, or just my youthful need for a tough challenge. If it was the latter, then fishing certainly had all the right ingredients. Leaving school at fifteen, I had started work in an antique shop with a view to learning the trade, but shop life was not for me. I craved fresh air and sunshine and the company of less devious, more straight- forward people.

As a hobby I had started to make a collection of old photographs of Looe, and during my lunch hour I used to wander around the quayside talking to the fishermen, trying to get boats and people in these photos identified. That was when I first met Frank Pengelly, the skipper of the lugger *Iris*. Climbing the vertical iron ladder up to his net loft above the old fish market, I would find him there overhauling the drift nets ready for the coming season. Watching Frank at work with the net needle, mending rents and tears in the nets, fascinated me, and it wasn't long before I was having a go, learning to mend 'bars' and 'three-ers'.

In conversation one day, we were talking about the antique trade. I mentioned that I was getting fed up with it, especially being stuck indoors. Having played around in boats most of my life, and having done those few trips out on the *One Accord*, the idea was growing in me that I might like going to sea on a full time basis. When I told Frank this, much to my amazement he offered me a berth on the *Iris* and from that moment there was no going back.

It was then that a battle royal began with Mum and Dad. I couldn't blame them for being somewhat hostile to the idea of this career change. I was in a job with regular wages and very good prospects, and I wanted to throw it all in to go fishing. Dad gave me the waggly finger, trying to impress upon me the fact that there was no future prospect in fishing. It was a dying trade, the wages were dreadfully uncertain and, what's more, he reckoned that I was never strong enough, or tough enough, to stick the long hours and harsh conditions worked in at sea. He was right on all points of course, but still I persisted, until eventually they caved in.

Permission was granted, but with the final rejoinder that I would be back in less than six months begging for my old job back. I must admit they were very nearly right on several occasions. Working out my last week at the antique shop seemed more like a month, but eventually Friday afternoon arrived, I picked up my last wage packet (£3.10) and cycled home with that wonderful end of term feeling.

Saturday morning saw me biking down to Polperro to buy oilskins and sea boots at Owen Goodland's hardware shop. Owen himself wasn't there, but he had opened his shop and a note on the door informed customers that he had gone out to his garden for the day and if anyone wanted anything, please help yourself, leave a note by the till of what you have had and come back and pay another day. This was typical of Owen; if there was anything more interesting to do than stay in his shop on a fine day, like gardening, fishing or greeting visitors in the street, he did it. His system seemed to work, even if he didn't. Pushing the shop door open, the spring bell jangled and I entered an establishment that seemed to sell just about everything. Clothes, artists' materials, bedding, lamp glasses and lino, carpets and crockery, 78rpm records, shoes, even garden produce, in fact anything you could think of, much of it so out of date or style that there was surely very little hope of ever finding customers for it. At the back of the shop I positioned the stepladder and helped myself to an oilskin jumper off of the top shelf. Next, by ferreting around in boxes and cupboards I found the other items that I needed: a sou'wester, sea boots and an oilskin apron. Leaving my name and a list for Owen, I strapped everything on the carrier of my bike and cycled back home to Talland Bay, feeling on top of the world. It was March 1964 and my new way of life was about to begin.

2

The *Iris* and her Crew

Sunday is the start of the fisherman's week, and four o'clock in the afternoon was sailing time on that particular Sunday. I made sure that I was aboard in good time. It was the long lining or 'boulter' season and Frank was working the Lizard ground.

To be honest, I don't remember a great deal about that very first trip other than, mercifully, it was flat calm. The lines were shot and hauled, and then I was put in the wheelhouse and given a landmark to steer for, while the rest of the crew were on deck clearing the lines back into the baskets. Steering the *Iris* meant standing up as there was no wheelhouse seat, and having been awake for many more hours than I was used to, I kept nodding off, only to wake with a start as my knees buckled and my head hit the wheelhouse window.

The catch was landed at Mevagissey as we had missed the tide for Looe. Tying up at the outer quay, the fish were pulled up, maund basket at a time, by a little crane that had been made out of an old line jinny. There it was weighed, boxed and stacked up on the fish merchant's truck, the boat was then scrubbed up from stem to stern before we all went ashore for fish and chips while awaiting the next tide up to Looe.

The catch must have made very good money, because the weather turned poor and we didn't get to sea for the rest of the week, but on Saturday, when the skipper shared the money out, I received £19 and being a learner, I was on half share. This was more money than I had ever had in one lump sum before. I was elated, but Dad was a bit miffed when I told him, as he only earned £18 for a full week as a skilled man.

In the fishing industry there has never been any such thing as a regular wage. The money grossed by the boat every week is shared out after the immediate expenses such as diesel have been deducted. One share for each member of the crew, one for the boat and one for the gear; big grossing big wages, no grossing no wages. When times were good, money had to be put by to see you through the lean times that were bound to come, and this meant a very frugal lifestyle had to be lead. At that time, hardly anyone could drive or owned a car, very few had TVs or telephones and holidays were a very rare treat. It was considered to have been a good year if all the bills were paid and there was a bit of money to spare for Christmas. Some skippers owned their own homes, but most fishing families rented a cottage or a council house where, if they had a spare room, the wife did bed and breakfast in the summer time. The only luxury enjoyed by the men was a pint of beer and a smoke, while the women ran the home and juggled the money.

The skipper of the *Iris*, Frank 'Moogie' Pengelly, was, at 43, the youngest and certainly the toughest skipper in the port. Of medium height and build, he was an amiable enough chap ashore, but at sea, stand back! And if, for some reason, he lowered his head and glared at you over the top of his glasses, you knew you were doomed.

The rest of the crew at the time included Bruce 'Tiddler' Sammels, 55-years-old and, apart from one summer away crewing on a yacht, he had been at sea on the luggers all his life. A jovial, easy-going fellow, he could neither read nor write, loved his beer and a pipe of black twist tobacco. It was said that he was the only fisherman in Looe fat enough to fill his oilskin jumper out, wrinkle free.

Next was Clarence Libby, a quietly spoken, gentlemanly type in his early 60s, but to me he looked nearer 80. He was bald, stooped, pale and frail-looking and speed-wise for working he never seemed to get out of first gear, but that gear was a very powerful one and conditions on deck had to be just about life threatening before he would give up and come down into the cabin. Clarence had spent much of his early working life as a sailor on square-riggers, schooners and big yachts which maybe accounted for his premature ageing.

Then came Jack Harris, a slight figure in his mid twenties. He had served for a number of years in the Royal Navy. A rogue with a great sense of humour, who seemed to live by one very simple creed, money was for spending, beer was for drinking and never, ever overlook an opportunity to get your leg over.

Then there was Harry 'Slender' Stevens, ginger haired and built like a Japanese racing snake. Harry was a baker by trade, but having suffered from TB in his early 40s, the doctors had advised him to get a light outdoor job. Now in his late 50s he had been on the *Iris* for some ten years acting as permanent 'boy' and ship's character.

Last of all myself, Paul Greenwood, aged 16, tall and skinny, as green as grass, with not an inkling of an idea of what I was in for.

Our good ship, the *Iris* (FY 357) was 44 feet long with a beam of 14 feet and a draught of six feet. She had been built in 1921 by the Looe shipwright, 'Young' Dick Pearce (not to be confused with 'Old' Dick Pearce, his father), upon the orders of Frank's father and grandfather to replace their little sailing lugger, the *Olive*. For a lugger she was a great lump of a boat, and carved on each bow and on the transom were the letters I.R.I.S. as she had been named after Frank's four aunts, Ida, Rosie, Irene and Suzie. Originally she had been an auxiliary, but the only sail she now carried was a gaff mizzen, used when working up to the nets and lines, or sheeted away to help on a run home with a fair wind.

She boasted three engines, all Lister diesels: a 45 HP situated in the aft cabin, and a 30 and a 21 HP down in the forepeak. The aft engine had an electric starter, while the two down forward had to be coaxed into life manually with handles and much sweating. All three engines were used when making a passage, but only the aft one was used when working to the gear. This had a throttle control inside the wheelhouse and a gear leaver out on deck for convenience when fishing. All three propellers emerged from the port quarter keeping the starboard side clear for working the nets and lines. She would come around to starboard in her own length, but needed the whole of Looe Bay to come around to port, but as it was considered unlucky to turn against the sun, this didn't matter. When all three engines were running, especially when making all speed to save tide into the harbour and the governors were lashed back, the deck seemed to undulate with the strain, and a turn and a half of port wheel was needed to keep her going in a straight line.

In the wheelhouse (besides the wheel working the chain steering) was a compass, a clock and an echo sounder. Despite having a wheel, tiller orders were still used when giving directions. Hard to port meant hard to starboard on the wheel; the boat went to starboard but the tiller, now only a stump at the rudder head, went to port. It could be very confusing.

The fishing industry in Cornwall at that time was at a very low ebb. Skippers had to maintain their boats and gear on a shoestring budget, and it was all make do and mend. There was nothing to spare to fund any improvements or modernisation and really, apart from having engines as the motive power instead of sails, the job and way of life had much more in common with the nineteenth century than the twentieth.

A lugger's 'safety equipment' consisted of a copper foghorn, usually kept in a cabin locker and rummaged out when needed, dripping verdigris and leaving a foul taste in the mouth of who ever had to blow it. A 'flare-up' consisted of a quart copper mug filled with paraffin which had a tight fitting lid that extended out to the size of a tea plate. On top of the lid was a handle, like the hilt of a sword, and when fitted on the mug a stout piece of wire six or eight inches long wrapped with rag extended down into the paraffin from the inside of the lid. When needed, the lid was taken off and the projecting rag was set alight. I suppose it could have been used to attract the attention of other boats if we were in trouble, but it's main function was to direct steamers away from the nets at night. This was achieved by waving it in a big slow circle in the direction you wanted them to go. In daylight, an oilskin was used in the same way. Ship to shore radios in those days were very expensive and were so big they would have taken up all the room in the wheel-house, which is why there was no radio communication.

First aid consisted of a bottle of whisky (usually kept wedged under the skipper's bunk) and clean engine room rags. A bad cut would have a drop of whisky poured on it before it was bound up. Mind you, some of the old boys would insist on having the tot poured down their neck rather than over any cut. In winter, if any one was 'nipped' by the cold, a tot would be dished out to them as they tried to warm up again, huddled over the cabin fire.

Safety was mainly achieved through years of experience and a high standard of seamanship. If you were in trouble, it was up to you to get out of it. Springing a leak in bad weather was one of the worst things that could happen. It was a rare occurrence, but over the years not a few boats have made it back to the safety of the harbour with one man swinging steadily on the pump, the rest of the crew manning a bucket chain.

I heard a story of one lugger that was making so much water they just could not keep her free so, to try and lessen the inrush, one of the crew sat on the leak and then his backside was caulked around with rags. This staunched things enough for the pump and buckets to deal with it. Leaks were usually caused by a plank end or butt, springing, caused by poor fastenings. On the next low tide, one of the local shipwrights would refasten, recaulk and putty the offending area, making her seaworthy once more.

At least with engines you could pretty much rely on getting back to your home port. Adverse conditions just entailed hours of fighting big cresting seas, hoping that the motors would keep going and the fuel last out, but hearth and home were beckoning. In the sailing days, when caught out in a bad blow, the boats would sometimes have to ride to their gear for days, unable to haul it. When the weather abated, the gear was hauled and a course was set for the nearest port, perhaps hailing a merchantman to get a position. Arriving at harbours anywhere from the Isle of Wight to the Scillies, news of their safe arrival would be telegraphed home, the fish sold and some food bought, before making a passage back to their home port.

The *Twilight* (FY 334) of Looe rode out such a gale, eventually making it home to Looe first go, five days after she left port. While anchoring in the bay to await tide into the harbour, a boy rowed out to meet her. Having been away for so long, the Navy had been alerted to keep a look out for them, but with no reported sightings, people were beginning to think the worst. After the boy blurted out "What happened to you, where did you get to, and is every one all right?" the skipper looked at him, saying, "Never mind all that, we have been living on boiled fish for days, I thought you would have brought us out a bag of buns or something."

In another incident, the *Kathleen* (FY 297) turned up at the Isle of Wight having weathered a snorter of a westerly gale, and the *Dove*, a misfit of a boat, known affectionately as the 'Sting Bum', took 30 hours to gain the shelter of Torbay, having rode to her nets for two days. That same boat was once blown away in a gale when fishing deep off the Lizard. Three days later she battled in to Falmouth, everyone and everything awash. They didn't even have a dry match to light the cabin fire with and as nobody had a penny on them, they hawked their fish around the windjammers anchored in the Carrick Roads, before tying up at Custom House Quay for some much needed rest and recuperation. The skipper of the *Dove* was Harold 'Nibbs' Butters, and one of her crew that told me the yarn was Edwin 'Snaker' Dann. I knew them both as old men; as characters they were worth their weight in gold, and you could safely say for 'rest and recuperation' read beer. Aboard the *Dove* on that trip was a boy out for the first time. As soon as they hit dry land he caught the train home to Looe and never went to sea again. With an introduction to fishing like that who can blame him.

None of the above trips should have lasted any longer than twelve hours if they were netting or, if lining, 24 to 30 hours. Back in their home port with the rain lashing and the wind howling down the chimney pots, the knowledge that one of the fleet was out there riding a gale must have been worrying in the extreme.

In the sailing days, being caught in a flat calm could be as trying as a gale of wind. The crew of the Mevagissey lugger *Erin* laboured at the sweeps for 20 hours to gain their home port from 40 miles out on the lining grounds. Her five-man crew did 20 minutes on each of the four sweeps, giving each man a spell on the tiller every hour and twenty minutes. By the same token, a Polperro gaffer, the *Mary*, had a man lying in the cabin collapsed with exhaustion by the time she poked her stem into harbour. When engines first became available the fishermen thought they were in heaven, as they made their lives so much easier.

3

Toughening Up

The Channel lining season continued until the pilchard shoals came on to the coast in more viable numbers around mid April. We would know when they arrived because to go long lining you need pilchards for bait and, to this end, a short fleet of nets was carried. Sometimes the nets would have to be shot and hauled twice to catch the 40 stone that was needed to bait up a long line, numbering six to seven thousand hooks stretched out on seven or more miles of back rope. If you were still short it might be possible to buy a few stone from one of the other boats. But if all failed, it was back to harbour and try again the next night. "With out any bait, you're bate" was the old saying.

On this particular night we went to work hauling the nets for line bait and ended up with about 150 stone of pilchards. 'Moogie' decided that was good enough, it was time to start the summer season. This was excellent news, for instead of ploughing out into the Channel for 24 hours hard graft, we were bound back to harbour to land our catch. Arriving in Looe just as dawn was breaking, the skipper roused out Gilbert Hocking, the fish canner's agent, to tell him that we had a catch of fish for them and that we were going to haul the main fleet of nets aboard to start the summer season.

The *Iris* was then moored up opposite her net loft above the old fish market. 'Tiddler' and Clarence went up and lowered down bundles of cork buoys and buffs ready to tie on the nets. The buoys were made up of 20 or so cork discs threaded on to a rope, each disc a good inch thick and about the size of a CD. The buffs were a mixture of old and new; the new were like big balloons made from heavy orange plastic, the old were made of canvas, tarred on the inside and painted white on the outside. Looking like monster footballs, the necks of them were fastened around a four-inch wooden disc in which was set a tapered bung. They were inflated with a big copper pump. Next, the end from the top of a heap of nets, all 'scunned' (tied) together ready to go, was passed down. The boat was slewed off the quay a few feet and we were ready to start. The new end was scunned on with 'tatchins' (short pieces of twine) to the bait fleet and these nets were first hauled through the water to wet them. Two men in the starboard waterways hauled aboard and stowed them in the net room, tying on buoys and buffs as they went. I was put in the port waterways with a deck bucket to throw more water on the skirt of the net to make sure it was good and sodden, and so sink away when shot.

When the job was complete, the lorry arrived with the fish boxes and all hands set to boxing up and landing the pilchards. All hands that is, except me. "Better give her a dig out," said 'Moogie'. So I went back to the pump, a big lead barrel affair with a see-saw handle set back against the aft net room bulkhead on the port side. To work the pump it first had to be primed with a bucket of water. You then jigged on the handle until it 'caught'. Then it was swing away steadily (discharging about a gallon per stroke) until it sucked air, indicating it was 'all out'. There I was, swinging the pump until my back was breaking and my arms were dropping off. I shouted for somebody to give me a 'spell' but was promptly told that, as I had put the water in her, I could get it out. I was learning.

After the fish were landed, and the baskets of line were put ashore, all hands set to with brooms and buckets to scrub the boat down. We were all ready to start the summer pilchard season. It was now lunchtime, and we had been working solidly since six o'clock the previous evening. What a relief it was to get our boots and oilskins off and head homewards.

But our relief was to be short lived. "Five o'clock tonight, boys," said the skipper as we traipsed off, looking forward to a wash, a meal and a few hours kip. We were all aboard again at the set hour and trooped down to the cabin to put our sea boots on, then back up on deck to make the boat ready for sea. 'Moogie' checked over and started the aft engine, while the rest of us unshipped and stowed the leg, likewise the net room and fish box hatches. Harry, the cook, lit the coal stove and put the kettle on. Ropes and fenders were handed aboard, the boat was swung out into the tide and away we went. The good lugger *Iris* began yet another season in her long career.

For the first two years that I went to sea, if the weather was a bit unkind, I could spew for England and this was such a night. There was a fresh south-west wind raising a lumpy sea, with sea bobs breaking here and there. The chimney of the cabin fire was sending out a good whiff, as were the engines, while a steady honk of stale fish and bilge was permeating up from below. I was feeling 'cruddy' well and truly, and it wasn't long before I was on my knees paying homage to Neptune over the lee rail. Sea-sickness knocks the stuffing right out of you. After the first bout. your temperature drops back to normal and for a while you feel quite recovered. If there's work to be done, you can drag yourself about the deck to do it, you might even perk up a bit and kid yourself that it's all over, and for the rest of the night you'll be fine. Many months later, when I did start to conquer the dreaded mal de mer, that is what would happen, but not at this stage of the game. Pretty soon that old qualmy feeling would return, then it only needed a good lungful of coal or diesel smoke to send me back on my knees clutching the lee rail, eyes streaming and sweltering red hot inside my oilskins, retching fit to turn inside out.

I was wiping my chin with my hat and trying to recover from just such a bout when Jack Harris, ever the joker, suggested that, if I should feel something tough and hairy in my throat when vomiting, I should swallow back quickly. "Why?" I croaked feebly. "Because it's probably your asshole!" he replied. "And if you ever fancy eating again, you're going to need it." The boat gave a mighty lurch and I clung to the rail with the foam in the waterways filling my boots. Jack was sitting on the companionway hatch, laughing until the tears rolled down his cheeks.

The gear was shot that evening with out any assistance from me - maybe I tottered around to help scrub down, I can't remember. By now the engines were silenced, the mizzen was set, and we were riding to the nets with a freshening wind. A drifter riding to her gear in a fresh breeze develops a very curious motion, a mile and a half of nets act like a big piece of elastic. The wind and sea drive the boat back and back, stretching out the elastic, until the strain overcomes the sea and she shoots forward with a plunging rocking motion. Oh, what misery.

Harry shouted "Tea up," so all hands went below for supper and maybe an hour in their bunks, but not me. I remember clearly sitting behind the wheelhouse on the cabin hatch trying to sip a mug of tea and nibble on a biscuit. Glancing down the cabin seeing the rest of the crew smoking and yarning, I was convinced that I would never be able to sit down there while at sea.

We rode to the nets for a couple of hours or so, then the aft engine was fired up, all hands pulled on their oilskins and hauling commenced. I was supposed to be helping 'Tiddler' back on the head ropes, but I was completely knackered. I could hardly help myself let alone help 'Tiddler', and the night seemed to go on for ever. Eventually the pole end net was hauled over the roller and 'Moogie' came aft to the wheelhouse and squared her away for home.

Oh, the relief when we got into the harbour, and better still when I got home and crawled into my bed. I can still recall that wonderful feeling of peace, safety and warmth after a night of undiluted misery. I suffered many more nights like that when the weather was bad, but gradually the seasickness became less severe and less frequent. Eventually it faded away, until I too could go down the cabin and have my supper on a rolling evening, but the whole procedure took about two years. But I knew I had really conquered the 'crud'.

The cabin itself had five bunks, three across the transom and one out each side forward of them. In front of the side bunks were seat lockers in which coal for the fire was kept. The fire was a miniature black lead range with an oven, where pasties were warmed and fish was baked. It was bolted down to the cabin sole over the gearbox coupling of the aft engine which had its own little engine room forward of the cabin but there was no bulkhead in between. In here, to starboard, was a 50 gallon diesel tank with a small leak; the drips were caught in an old cake tin. To port, in their box, were the batteries for the lights, plus the engine oil tank and half a dozen hurricane lamps used on the danns. Under the fore end of the engine was the pump well where the bilge water drained. This was a mixture of oil and diesel leaking from the engines, along with decaying fish and muck draining out of the nets. At sea with the hatch open, the bilge pumped out, the fire alight and the engine running, it was pretty hot down there but the smell didn't seem too bad. It was when working from other ports and the cabin became our home, we had the full benefit of its charms. The covering board in the area of the bunk that I was given leaked so much that the old flock bedtide (mattress) would make a fizzing noise when you hit it. I turfed that out and lined the whole bunk with polythene and then invested in a new bedtide.

When we were all turned in, the weather boards shipped up and the hatch was shut tight, the only ventilation available was the nor-wester. This was a small hatch in the forward bulkhead that slid open to reveal the net room. For five or six hours the aromas would amalgamate and concentrate (like a good stew): bilge water, coal and tobacco smoke, diesel and paraffin, the hot oil smell of the engine, stale sea boot socks plus the anal trumpeting of the sleeping crew.

The first man up always stirred up the fire and put the kettle on for tea, then slid back the cabin hatch to air things out a bit. It's no exaggeration to say that you could have cut the fug in the cabin into chunks and thrown them up on deck. Description does not do the stench of that cabin justice; it's something you just had to experience.

Harry Stevens went into the fishing late in life, which is probably why he never really had the physical strength or quickness of hand needed to work on the nets. But he was as tough as old boots, which is more than could have been said about me at the time. So until I got some sea legs and toughened up a bit, Harry had to go 'out the rail' and toil the best he could, while I did his job, and what a job that was! If there was a decent bit of fish coming aboard you didn't have time to draw breath.

'Tiddler' hauled and stowed the head ropes; his position was at the aft end of the starboard waterways, just in front of the wheelhouse. My place was to stand behind him, and as he came to a buoy rope he would toss a bight of it over his head. I had to haul the cork buoy aboard and stow it neatly down the net room out the starboard wing, with the buffs going to port, but that was only part of it. The man 'out the rail' would shout, "Go ahead," and I would tug on the lever to put the engine in gear to nudge the boat along the nets. The stower would shout, "Net room," and I had to jump down and pick up a pilchard that had been flipped onto the nets, scrambling up from there just in time to stow the next buoy and work the dip net. This was like a giant prawn net, used to dip up pilchards that had dropped from the nets as they were being hauled. Gulls in their hundreds would be trying to rob the nets, swooping and screaming, wings flapping in your face, feet tap-tapping on your hat as one held station awaiting his moment to dive shrieking into the melee. Scaring them off was also part of the brief, done by shouting and hollering at the top of your voice while whirling a buoy above your head. An awful lot of effort for never more than two minutes peace.

The pump had to be swung regularly as gallons of water were draining out from the nets, then it's time to nip down into the cabin to bank up the fire, appearing back on deck in time to adjust the mizzen and wheel to keep the boat at the right angle to the nets. On and on it went, relentlessly until the last net was hauled aboard, six, eight or even ten hours non-stop; even the boy's job was tough.

That was my lot for a couple of months, then one evening 'Moogie' told me I was going 'out the rail' and Harry was having his job back. He was more than welcome to it. This was definitely a step towards becoming a fully-fledged member of the crew and earning 'full share'.

The men crewing on the drifters were exceptionally strong, and possessed incredible endurance, because everything was achieved by 'Armstrong's patent'. As a learner, it took a long time to gain the strength needed for the job, and much suffering after that to find the necessary endurance. Hauling and dragging non-stop for hour after hour took some getting used to. At times I would feel so hungry I felt that I might collapse. Eventually that sensation would pass off, leaving the stomach feeling red hot. When that stage had been reached I knew I could go on for many more hours with no further trouble; a few boiled sweets tucked in the fold of my hat and snatched into my mouth when chance arose helped a fair bit.

As for thirst, well 'spitting feathers' would not have been an exaggeration. A gallon can of water was kept behind the wheelhouse and passed around when on a long haul, but that was no more than a couple of mouth's-full in perhaps eight or ten hours. When conditions demanded we sometimes worked for 30 or 40 hours straight, kept going with the odd mug of tea and bite to eat when the job in hand allowed.

By now, I was starting to gain some strength. I could swing the pump without my back breaking, shoot my share of nets without my arms turning to jelly, lift five stone boxes of fish about, and lay-to on the engine starting handles. Mind you, I was still battling with seasickness. Personally, I thought I was coming on in leaps and bounds, so it came as a great shock when I first went 'out the rail' to haul the nets aboard, helped by the second hand when needed. I got into position, caught hold of the net, braced myself and hauled, and I hauled again and nothing happened. I just couldn't move it. The skipper, as second hand on the skirt, stood behind me and he did the hauling with my arms moving in time, just like a puppet.

The other task was shaking the pilchards out. The net is hauled aboard until the stower shouts stop. He is the last one on the line, so when he has fish to shake out, everyone has. The fish were then shaken, flipped and twisted out of the meshes, preferably without tearing their heads off or ripping the net, and when the stower cleans out his bit of net, up it comes again. Well, I just didn't have the knack and my hands weren't tough enough. When trying to flip fish out with finger and thumb as shown, I either tore the mesh or the twine cut my finger joints open. Trying to twist them out, the heads came off, or the razor sharp bones just behind the gills known as collar studs cut my hands open.

All the while 'Moogie' was behind me saying, "Rattle your dusters, my sonny, a quick hand for a scabby arse," or else, "Up she comes, John Edward is looking at you". John Edward Hoskin had been the skipper of the lugger John Wesley (FY35) and both he and his crew had become a legend on the Cornish coast for the amount of fish they caught and the atrocious weather conditions they would put to sea in.

By the time the pole end buoy came over the roller, my back was breaking, my arms felt as if they were pulled out of their sockets and my hands were cut to raw liver. But I was put there the next night and the night after that, and there I stayed. I suppose there was no other way. Gradually I hardened up to the job, until one night I realised I could do it. "Up!" Clarence, the stower, would shout and when I laid back on the net, up it came, with very little help from the second hand. "Stop!" would come the order, and I could flip and twist the pilchards out of the mesh without an eighth of the damage done to my hands or the fish, and what was more, I was now on a full share of wages.

The money was always shared out on Saturday. All the crew would be down aboard by nine o'clock to get on with any jobs that needed doing. Someone would push the net cart up to the coal yard on Station Road to get fuel for the fire. Harry scrubbed out the cabin, black-leaded the stove and shopped for stores, the engines were greased up and checked over. Diesel was carried out from the fuel store in five gallon drums to be tipped into the tanks through a big copper funnel. There were always nets of different mesh sizes to haul in or out of the boat as the season changed. Around midday the skipper would call us up in order of seniority and pay out the share money at the wheelhouse door, having spent half an hour or so working it out on the back of an envelope with a stub of pencil. Then, when all the jobs were done, and the *Iris* was ready for the coming week. A time was set for the Sunday evening sailing, and the rest of the weekend was your own.

4

Teatime

The summer holiday season was now approaching and Clarence, our stower, had left us to work his ferry boat. He was getting on in years and only sailed with us in the spring and autumn to shorten up what would have been a very long winter for him. Clarence had a wonderful collection of sea jumpers from all the different vessels he had sailed on as a young man. Each one had the ship's name embroidered across the chest, and every jumper could bring forth a whole raft of stories.

Tales of when he was an AB on a barque transporting mature trees in tubs to a villa development on a Greek island, the trees so tall they couldn't set the courses (lower sails). Another ship on which he crewed, the mate had a pet monkey which he would send down below to rouse the next watch; the animal would bite and scratch the men out of their bunks, getting them up on deck in record time.

If anyone was feeling poorly, be it a hangover, a cold, 'flu, constipation or the opposite, Clarence had the one sovereign remedy. Looking at the sufferer a bit sideways, eyes twinkling and with the start of a smile on his face, he would say, "What you need, my sonny, is a good drag through with a holly bush."

The thing that always intrigued me about Clarence was his grub tin. It was a work of art. Everyone else had doorstop sandwiches or a pasty, slabs of cake and a packet of biscuits or, in 'Tiddler's' case, yards of boiled tripe and crackers plus plenty of stomach powders. Not so Clarence. His wife packed him immaculate little sandwiches with the crusts cut off, delicate slices of fruit cake and neat wedges of jam sponge, all wrapped in white linen serviettes. He took his tea from a bone china cup and saucer decorated with gold edging

46

and red roses, complete with a silver apostle spoon. When placed alongside our chipped tea-stained pint mugs to be filled, Harry had to squint hard through his glasses and take great care not to wash Clarence's cup into the bilge when tipping the tea from the gallon teapot.

With this in mind, you might easily imagine his wife to be a small, delicate, quiet little person. Not so. May was a big raw-boned farmer's wife type of woman, an ex-rowing champion with probably one of the loudest voices in the town. When we were working on East Looe quay, May would shout to tell her beloved his dinner was ready and we and the rest of the town could hear her loud and clear, and that was from their house which was up behind St. Nicholas' church at West Looe. A damned good shout away.

There was an old sailor man's riddle that Clarence used to put to anybody he thought may not have heard it. Being the boy aboard, I was open to all the old jokes and wheezes, but this was maybe one of the better ones:

> The wind was west
> And West steered we.
> If the sails did draw
> How could that be?

Well, I had one hand pointing to represent the wind, the other for the boat, and couldn't come up with an explanation that made any sense and had to give up. The answer was that West was the name of the skipper.

Clarence was a natural gentleman, quietly spoken and always polite. The man who took his berth for the summer was Jack Moore, ex-middleweight boxing champion of the navy. Jack was in his mid 50s and as strong as an ox. His hands were like sledge hammers and his nose was battered all over his face. He played an accordion, and on fine evenings he would bring it to sea, giving us a few tunes while we were riding to the gear. He was of an easy going nature and loved his pint, as did 'Tiddler', and quite often they would have a few before coming to sea. Then look out. The pair of them could agree on nothing and would be back aft shouting and arguing over the daftest things, until 'Moogie' told them to shut up. Many years later, when Jack was in his mid 70s, he was making his way home, having spent the evening babysitting for one of his sons, when two of

47

the local yobs tried to mug him. One ended up unconscious, having first been propelled by a swift left hook over a privet hedge, and the other was dangled by the scruff of the neck until Jack got him into the light to identify him. The shocked youth yelped for mercy and forgiveness until eventually Jack let him go. I rather imagine grand-dads were off the mugging list after that incident.

Fishing was good that spring. We worked long hard hours and made some very good wages. The biggest catch of the season went to the *Our Daddy*. She netted 1,500 stone of pilchards in one night - that's ten tons!

The summer evenings were fine and warm and the luggers from Looe and Mevagissey, not forgetting Polperro's *One Accord* were out searching for the pilchard shoals, trying to 'raise a scry' as it was called. If fish were scarce, the boats might end up close together on whatever sign there was; in the light evening air you could hear their crews talking, and the clatter of the pawl on the rail roller as they hauled their nets. On other occasions the shoals could be found anywhere, and the boats would hardly be in sight of one other. When the shoals were located, the boat was steamed up wind of them, then turned around and downwind we would go, with the shooting roller rattling as the nets went over the side, arm over arm at a spanking pace.

'Tiddler' would be at the wheel keeping the wind fine on the port quarter and knocking the engine in and out of gear to maintain a steady speed. 'Moogie' always shot the head ropes and threw the first or pole end buoy away to the cry of "God speed the plough", tossing the buoy and buff ropes back over his head for Harry to catch and pull out of the net-room to hurl them overboard with a splash. The first or pole end net was shot away, then came the dann with its hurricane lamp to mark the end of the fleet for other shipping. The skirt or foot of the nets was the hardest part to shoot, being wet heavy cotton net some eight fathoms deep and a third longer than the head-ropes, so we took turns, shooting four or five nets each, unless of course someone was feeling really perky and they stood there and shot the lot. We all did that at times, why I can't say, it was just how the mood took you.

Towards the end of the last net, the boat would be just creeping along, and as the final buoy went over the side, the wheel was put down hard to starboard, bringing her head to wind. The mizzen was hoisted, and the swing rope (the rope that attached the boat to the nets) was paid out and made fast on the bow kevel. "Stop engine," was the next order, and there we lay peacefully drifting with the wind and tide for the next two or three hours. Before we had our supper, buckets and brooms came into action to scrub down the bulwarks, deck and net-room. The big rail roller and shaking out spars were shipped up, ready for the haul while Jack Harris, as engine driver, greased up the shaft bearings or plummer-blocks as they were called.

Helping Jack to lift up the net room boards (they were two inches thick and as heavy as lead) to get at the plummer-blocks, I once remarked on their stoutness and was told that in 1940 many of the Cornish boats had been ordered to assemble at Plymouth's Millbay docks to be made ready to go to Dunkerque. That was when the heavy boards were fitted. But by the time the fleet was ready it was all over and they were stood down. Everyone breathed a sigh of relief and went home again.

When things were all shipshape on deck, it would then be time for supper, and a mug of tea. Harry's tea was unique, and very much an acquired taste; on occasions the making of it could be quite a pantomime. Our cook loved a drop of scrumpy and would very often indulge himself before coming to sea. This would make him rather drowsy or, if rubbed the wrong way, very argumentative. His first task on board was to light the fire and put the kettle on to boil. Into the firebox of the range would go paper, sticks and coal, then a good slop of diesel from the engine leak off bottle. A match was applied and away it would go. The kettle was then filled and placed on the range to boil. All was in order, so now was the time to have a little nap. But sometimes he napped for just that bit too long, and when he awoke the fire would be out; everything hot but the fire out. Now it's panic, the tea won't be ready on time and as poor old Harry used to have enough bollockings from the skipper as it was, any extras were to be avoided if at all possible. Into the firebox would go more paper, sticks and coal, plus another really generous slop of diesel. By the time he had fumbled about and put a match to it the range was a mass of diesel fumes, there would be a loud WHUMP sort of noise accompanied by much clattering and swearing. All hands would rush aft to the companionway and, peering down, the cabin would be full of smoke and soot. The range had exploded, blowing off its door and rounders, plus Harry's hat and glasses.

We all knew what had happened - we had seen it all before, as had the skipper who ducked out of the wheelhouse to see if Harry had managed to blow the stern end of the boat right off this time. "Harry, you bloody old fool, you've done it yet again!" 'Moogie' bellowed down into the smoke. Our cook, now as sober as a judge, would go into auto apologise mode, repeating "Sorry skip, sorry skip," as he groped around the cabin for his glasses in order to see to put the wreckage of the stove back together again. Providing you weren't down the cabin when it happened, this was fine entertainment and afterwards, watching Harry's cringe-worthy performance as he tried to act the part of the perfect deckhand/cook, only added to the fun.

Barring explosions, this was how the tea was made. Into the gallon teapot went four tablespoons of tea, and as many of sugar followed by the water (sometimes it might even be boiling). Plenty of condensed milk was then stirred in, and the pot placed back on the range to keep hot until needed. A brown scum always formed on top, plastering the inside of the mug and clinging to your top lip as you drank. The tea mugs were washed once a week when the cabin was scrubbed out, and by then the only clean place on them was where your lip touched the rim.

With daylight still in the sky we sat around the aft deck yarning and enjoying our bit of supper, the wind a light westerly over a tranquil sea, the land aglow, bathed in warm evening sunshine. On such an evening there was nowhere else you would rather be. When supper was over it was time to have a go with the hand lines before it got too dark. This was great sport. These lines consisted of about 50 fathoms of cod-line wound onto a wooden square, a brass swivel joined on a fathom of gut holding four hooks, ending with a 1lb lead. They were baited up with strips of pilchard to fish on the seabed 30 or 40 fathoms down as we drifted along. Whiting was the main catch, fine big fish coming up three or four at a time if we happened to drift over the right ground. We also caught pollack, ling, cod and hake, even the odd conger. Sometimes enough were caught to sell to the fish jowters to make a bit of stocker money; at other times there was just enough for a feed each. If that was the case, the fish were always shared out evenly back in harbour, just before we went home. 'Tiddler' would divide the fish into little heaps on the net-room hatches as fairly as he could, one for each member of the crew. Then, appointing one man to turn his back to it, 'Tiddler' would point to a pile of fish and ask him, "Who's shall this be?" and a crewman was named … and so on until everyone had been named and all had their share of fish. Bait for the lines was always cut up on the bait board. This was an ordinary piece of deal about eighteen inches by eight. There was a ritual joke attached to this board which I think held good on all the luggers, and it went like this. If you wanted to cut up some bait for your line and someone had just finished using it, or if you looked about and couldn't see it, you would of course say, "Pass me the bait board," or "Where is the bait board?" and it was passed over, or you were told where it was. But if you said, "Where's the board?" or "Pass me the board," the reply was always "What board?" and the answer had to be "The board the monkey fucked the cat on." With that, it was yours. As far as I can make out, that ritual had continued for generations and never failed to raise a smile.

Another old joke was the lighthouse on the pilchard's head. Slicing up some bait one evening, 'Tiddler' passed me over a pilchard. "There, boy," he said, "can you see the lighthouse on the pilchard's head?" Look as hard as I might, I couldn't see a lighthouse, knowing this was yet another old wheeze, but it was the first one I had come across where the main prop was a dead fish. Admitting defeat, I passed it back to 'Tiddler' who then pointed out a tiny marking on top of the pilchard's head, right between the eyes. Sure enough, it looked just like a miniature lighthouse. Giving the fish back, I was then told to look for the dog. Again, I had to give in. "I can't see a dog anywhere," I said. "No you won't, either," said 'Tiddler', puffing on his pipe as hard as he could to conceal his growing mirth. "Because he's around the other side of the lighthouse having a shit!" Caught again, to gales of laughter from the rest of the crew.

We had many enjoyable hours with the hand lines, especially if there was a bit of a jape to be played. If someone left their line unattended for a while, that was the time to whip it up a few fathoms, tie on a length of fine black mending twine and lower away again, leading the twine back around the boat where it couldn't be seen. When the angler returned and took hold of his line, the prankster would tug on the twine. "Ha, there they are, I can feel them," says the dupe. Tug, tug, again on the twine. "Come on, my beauties."

Tug, tug. "Right, my lovelies, up you come," and hand over hand, up it comes. If all went well he doesn't notice the mending twine and the hooks come up with only the bait on. "Well look at that," squeaks the victim. "Tugging like fuck they were, and the bastards have all got off!" Meanwhile, in the gloaming, five pairs of shoulders are heaving in silent mirth.

One of the old five stone aluminium fish cans hitched on to someone's line was always a good lark. It would shear about very convincingly when being hauled, bringing forth talk of big ray or turbot, and demands for someone to stand by with the gaff. Happy days!

When it got too dark for the hand lines, they were wound up and put away. Somebody might go below to snatch an hour in his bunk, others would remain kneeling on the deck, leaning on the rail quietly yarning, watching the lights along the shore and enjoying a smoke. 'Moogie' was usually in the wheelhouse looking at the echo sounder showing the pilchard shoals steadily ascending to feed in the dark plankton-rich surface water. You could hear them rattling and splashing around the boat. If the signs were looking good our captain would perk up no end, bursting into the odd verse of 'Nelly Dean' or 'Sweet Adeline' and, if he was feeling really great, that might well be accompanied by a spot of tap dancing. In the confines of that tiny shelter, and wearing sea-boots, it couldn't have been easy.

As soon as he judged the time was right we would hear the shout, "Right ho, boys, get ready". The starter whined and the aft engine burbled into life, boots and oilskins are pulled on ready for the haul to begin. 'Moogie' would go forward to the swing rope and order a touch ahead on the engine to take the weight off it, and we would haul away, coiling it down on the net room boards. When the swing rope was up short, it was passed back to the head rope man who then pulled in the last couple of fathoms to the net. The rail man then took hold of the end lining and pulled away to get it all on deck. He got it 'laying fair' then hauled again to pass it back to the second hand, and so on back to the stower.

We were now all ready to start the haul. "Go ahead five," shouts the rail man. Harry shoves the engine into gear and counts five, enough in fine weather. If the fishing is steady and the pilchards spaced fairly evenly along the net, the man 'out the rail' just hauled away steadily and shouted "Ahead five" every now and then to keep the boat up to the nets, while the pawl on the rail roller clattered away merrily. The men behind him shook and flipped the fish out of the net, while the stower cleared out a few scads and mackerel plus the odd conger drill, keeping the rhythm going. We might not make our fortunes that night, but there was a 'little blessing' and it would all add up at the end of the week.

After five or so hours of easy hauling, the nets were 'all in' and we would now be heading homeward. Jack Harris and I would nip down forward and crank the '30' into life and give it half throttle, then get back up on deck to help unship the roller and spars, stow the mizzen and box the catch up ready to land. There was no time for another cup of tea, for we would soon be back in harbour.

As we enter Looe bay off Hannafore, Jack would nip down forward and the ease the '30' down and stop as we enter harbour in the soft light of early dawn. At the quayside, ropes and fenders are put out and the leg shipped up. Jack Moore would drag the balance scales and weights out of the shed and set them up. Meanwhile the rest of us would chuck the boxes of fish ashore for 'Moogie' and Harry to weigh and stack up ready for the lorry to take them to the cannery at Newlyn, 120 stone in all.

Buckets and brooms were plied to give the old boat a good scrub up, along with our oilskins and boots. Anything in contact with the pilchards got lagged in scales. When all was clean and tidy, it was time for home. "Same time tonight, boys," said our skipper, as we headed off for breakfast and a few hours kip.

Hauling away one evening, the conditions were just as I have described. 'Tiddler' was looking down at a bunch of gulls that were fighting over a fish, his 'chickens' he always called them. In his chicken voice, a high falsetto, he clucked and scolded at them for being so ill mannered. "I'll give the missis a telling off when I get home," he announced to the rest of us. "I told her to lock them up at sunset, and now they're out here playing up hell." Then he went back to clucking and scolding. Maybe it was the thought of his wife, the voluptuous Gwen, waiting for him at home in bed, I don't know, but all of a sudden, after a period of silence, he was groping at the front of his oilskin and bellowing loudly to be taken ashore. "What the hell is the matter with you 'Tiddler'?" said Moogie. "Would you believe it," came the reply "Gwenie's pride hasn't stood to attention for two years, now he's up like a ramrod, and I'm out here. Get me ashore Moogie, get me ashore!"

5

Sleeping

All the crew except myself lived within ten minutes walk of the quay in Looe. Talland Bay was two and a half miles away and for 18 months or so, until I bought a motorbike, I walked or push-biked there and back. Being young this didn't worry me; the walk took three quarters of an hour; by bike, 25 minutes. The trouble was that the bikes never lasted very long. Because it was much the quickest route, half the journey home was down a very rough lane, deeply rutted and made up with lumps of stone as big as your fist. Going down it in daylight was no problem, but in the dark, guided only by looking up at the lighter sky between the high hedges (lights never stayed working for very long) was a recipe for punctured tyres, buckled wheels and many a spill.

Attempts to sleep during the day were not always very successful. Everyone else was up and about doing their thing, while I was trying to get some rest. Many a time I gave up, going to sea in the evening dog tired and, as 'Tiddler' would say, "With eyes like sheep's cunnie's".

Often it was possible to have a nap on the way out to shoot the nets, and a couple of hours could usually be had while riding to them. When dog-tired, what utter bliss it was to climb into my bunk and lay there dozing, warm and comfortable. But no matter how tired I was, when it was time to turn out you had to be out on the instant, pronto. If someone gave you a shout or shook you, or if steaming and the engine was eased down, there was no time allowed to come to gently and pull your thoughts together. It was out of your bunk and up on deck the very instant of being roused, and woe betide anyone who was slow. I well remember taking time crawling out of my bunk when I first started, to receive one hell of a bollocking. "You idle little bastard, you'll die in your bunk if you carry on like that. The fog might have come down, a steamer might be about to ram us, you don't know what might be happening," yelled 'Tiddler'. "The next time I give you a shake, out of your fucking bunk and up on the bastard deck straight away." It was hard training but it was just. There were one or two men in the fleet who had had some terrible experiences in the navy during the war: they were shaken with a broom handle to rouse them because they would sometimes come out of the bunk fighting for their life.

On the *Iris*, unless you could sleep with one eye open it was not a good idea to nod off sitting on the cabin lockers - there were too many jokers about. Some poor bugger, utterly exhausted, slumped in a corner of the cabin 'driving the pigs home', was likely to end up with his feet tied together, hat made fast with mending twine to a nail in the deck head and his face decorated with soot from the fire to resemble an Indian on the warpath. It happened to us all over the years. Of course, when the shout goes up to get on deck, there's the victim, only semi-conscious, lunging for the companionway wondering why his feet won't work and what has happened to his hat. The best bit would be if he didn't realise that he had been done up with the soot so that, after sorting out feet and hat, 'Geronimo' would take his place on deck. Sooner or later he would say or do something that, combined with the war paint, would make him look utterly ridiculous. Half an hour or so of pent up sniggering would burst forth in a tidal wave of laughter, and the game was up. Bent over a bucket of sea water trying to clean up a bit, tongue-in-cheek revenge was top of the agenda: "You think that's funny, just wait till I catch one of you bastards asleep. In fact, don't any of you nod off for the next six months!"

At sea one night, we had a bit of unexpected excitement, courtesy of the Royal Navy. It all began with the *Iris*'s electrical system. The wiring for this was not of the best, the lights were operated from a number of old domestic switches, screwed at random to the deck head of the wheelhouse and joined up with anything from light flex to cooker wire. If a tall man was at the wheel, he had to stand at the stoop or else, as the boat rolled, his hat would brush the switches, turning the lights on and off. On this particular evening we were laying to the nets and 'Moogie' couldn't get the riding lights to work, so a Tilley lamp was rigged forward in their stead.

It was a calm, quiet evening and as black as pitch. We were all sat aft smoking and yarning when presently we heard the thrum of powerful engines but couldn't make out the vessel as she too had her lights out. Suddenly we were in the glaring beam of a searchlight, and a megaphone voice quacks, "Drifter, please display the correct lights, as it is confusing to other mariners," to which someone shouted back, "Where the fuck's yours?" We were being paid a visit by the Fishery Protection boat.

Meanwhile our skipper's third rendition of 'Sweet Adeline' had been hastily curtailed and he was now furiously twiddling wires to try and get some lights working. Eventually on came the riding lights, followed by the working lights and an order to "Get ready". It wasn't long before we were hauling away, but to our great discomfort the fishery boat was still hovering about. Suddenly there was a dinghy at our port side, with two ratings and a young officer aboard. The officer awaited his moment, and as the old *Iris* rolled to port, he nimbly jumped aboard to near disaster. The net-room was nearly empty, and the port waterways were very narrow. What he expected as he leaped, I don't know, but luckily he did just manage to pitch in the waterways and not down into the net-room; it left him totally unbalanced, gyrating and snatching at the air, like an epileptic disco dancer. When his balance and dignity were somewhat restored, he strutted aft and stood there, full of 'piss and importance'. We carried on working meanwhile, taking no notice of him at all. Forward he came again: "Who's the skipper?" he barked. Frank had to confess that he was, and dropped the net to go aft and give our details. When the officer was satisfied that we were up to nothing illegal, he returned to the mine-sweeper and it departed. Later, Frank admitted he had been very tempted to name Harry as the skipper, but after the officer's undignified boarding he didn't reckon his sense of humour would have stretched that far.

6

Local Characters

Looe was not an easy port to work from, built as it is on a narrow tidal river. On a spring tide the water flows in and out at an alarming pace and the boats have to be handled with great skill if the skippers are to avoid doing any damage and suffer a severe loss of dignity. When the wind is in the easterly quarter, a nasty bar can build at the entrance, requiring deft boat handling to pass safely over it. At neap tides, it's low water in the morning and evening, and the boats had to anchor in the bay.

This is where the 'scruffer' came in. Scruffing was, and still is, the name given to the job of attending to the boats when they are anchored off, and the scruffer was one of a band of retired fishermen who supplemented his pension by working a small boat on the harbour ferry or doing river trips in the summer. In the early 1960s that post was held by Albert the Belgie. He and his family had escaped to Looe from Ostend on his trawler when the Germans overran Belgium in WW2. Albert's ferry boat, the good ship *Nancy D*, was not exactly the best in its class; the engine would splutter to a halt on a regular basis due to overheating or the plug sooting up, but he always managed to coax it into life again. It was the same for everyone in those days, make do and mend.

On neap tides when the luggers *Guide Me*, *Iris*, *Our Boys*, the *Our Daddy* and 'Lishy' Soady's quatter *Endeavour* would be anchored in the bay, mizzens set and looking to the west as pretty as a picture, their crews assembling at the sea front smoking and yarning, Albert would be waiting off the pier in his boat, jigging on the pump and hoping that his engine was in a good mood. 'Moogie' would come jaunting out, grub tin under his arm.

"Everyone here?" he asked. "Yes," came the reply, "but hang on a minute, 'Tiddler' has gone for a piddle." With that, 'Tiddler' appeared. "With a gut like you've got you can't have seen the end of your cock for years," comes somebody's kind remark. "I'm going on a diet, then things will be different," he replied as he waddled down the pier with us, having just put five pints of Bass down his neck, his grub tin, as always, stuffed full of boiled tripe and crackers.

Albert saw us coming and poked his boat alongside the pier steps while we tumbled down the granite treads and climbed aboard. The tired old engine was shoved into gear and out into the bay we went, well nearly … the engine coughed and stopped dead. "Help, help, shipwreck, we are all going to drown," someone shouted in mock terror, "Get the oars out, we'll row her," is another helpful suggestion. "Christ, he'll even want paying in a minute," said 'Moogie' with a wink.

But Albert Diems was 'Mr Cool', and a man of very few words. He had witnessed the horrors of WW1, he had battled winter gales trawling in the North Sea and finally, in WW2, he and his family had been bombed and machine-gunned by the invading Germans and exiled from their country. Nothing that happened here in Looe could even slightly advance his heart rate, let alone alter his facial expression. If he did speak, it was only to answer 'Moogie' who always asked him, "What do you know Albert?" and the reply was always, "Fuck all". End of conversation.

Impassively, he cleans the spark plug and cranks the engine up again. This time we made it out to the lugger, and Albert got his money.

With the aft engine ticking over, the skipper nudged the boat along the anchor road. It was cable laid manila, as thick as your wrist and stiff with tar. I was down in the forepeak coiling it onto the cable tier while the others were hauling. When the anchor was stowed, Jack came down and we cranked up the '30' and the '21' and gave them half throttle. Back up on deck we help the others to unship the net-room and fish box hatches, then ship up the shooting roller and drop the mizzen peak. The cabin chimney was billowing evil-smelling smoke, indicating that Harry was having some success with the fire. The four other boats were not far behind us, it was a fine summer evening and the Looe fleet was off to sea once more.

Harry, our little wiry, ginger-haired cook was a widower. He lived in a cottage in the old part of town known as the 'Back Streets'. Nicknamed 'Scrumpy' Harry after his favourite beverage, or 'Harry Slender' because of his slight build, he was the only member of the crew who could drive. His transport was a bubble car, the type where the whole front of the vehicle hinged back, and up to three people could climb in and perch on the bench seat within. It would get you from A to B, but any 'cool' you might have possessed, evaporated the very instant you got in to it. I well recall the time he gave it a coat of paint. No preparation was deemed necessary, he just slapped it on with a hairy cow's tail of a brush. The paint he used was from a jammy old tin of cream-coloured stuff that he had found up the net loft. Textured, I suppose, was the best way to describe the finish, especially after little whorls of wind had liberally coated it with grit and toffee papers.

Regardless of the paint job, Harry was proud of his vehicle, and it played a vital role when he went a-courting. Over the years, he had squired various widows around the area, and when setting forth on one of these hot dates, we would see him resplendent in his best courting rig. It consisted of a white shirt, with a red and blue cravat, blue/green drainpipe trousers, white winkle picker shoes (brogue pattern) and a blue blazer with a flower in the buttonhole, topped off with a green Tyrolean hat with a pheasant's tail feather set at a jaunty angle in the band. A silver handled cane and gold framed monocle, completed his raffish air. Thus suitably attired, and fortified with a few pints of the best farmhouse scrumpy, he would board his trusty steed and putter off for a dirty weekend.

We were riding to the nets one evening and everyone was sitting down in the cabin having supper and yarning when the subject of Harry's most recent weekend away came up. Of course we started to tease him a bit: "Come on, Harry, tell us how it went." "Did you rise to the occasion?" and so on. With that, he gets his wallet out of his back pocket and from it produces a tiny wrap of cigarette paper, inside of which, tied around with cotton, was a tuft of pubic hair. "There you are," he said, holding it up to his nose between thumb and forefinger, eyes closed as he savoured the delicate aroma. "Wonderful." With that, it was passed from hand to hand for all to appreciate, while he regaled us with his weekends exploits. At least four more such trophies were produced for our delectation. It was like a surreal wine evening, the vintner passing around his finest wines and telling proudly of their history.

On one occasion, the landlord of the Looe Hotel gave Harry a huge, very over-ripe gorgonzola cheese that would have taken him about a fortnight to eat. Down in the cabin it whiffed away menacingly in his grub tin. With the boat riding quietly to the nets, we would be sitting around the cabin fire enjoying our supper and a yarn until Harry decided to make some inroads into this cheese and took the lid off his tin. The stench was eye watering, breathtaking, instantly causing the crew of the *Iris* to be jammed three deep in the companionway, fighting to get up on deck. Meanwhile the man himself, oblivious to the chaos he was causing, was busy piling mounds of this decaying dairy produce onto cracker biscuits, and savouring every mouthful. He got away with this performance for a couple of nights. Eventually 'Moogie' stuck his head down the hatch, eyes watering with the up rush of ammonia fumes, and diplomatically requested he dispose of it. His exact words being, "Harry, for fuck's sake heave that bloody thing overboard".

Harry was a character extraordinaire, with a mind set all of his own. So many years have passed since those days, but I still chuckle to myself when I recall some of his antics, and the yarns he spun.

7

Sharking

In the days before foreign holidays became popular, Cornwall in the summer months used to be packed to the gunwales with people on their annual fortnight's holiday. Looe would ring to the sound of Welsh, Brummie and a whole variety of other regional accents as different industries shut down for their annual vacations. Most people arrived by train and spent much of their time in the town or on coastal walks, coach trips, shopping for nick-knacks, boozing, beaching and boating. Sea angling, especially shark fishing, was very popular and as a result about 20 boats, both large and small, earned a good living with the rod and line. At the height of the season, during the school holidays, these boats just couldn't cope with the numbers of people wanting a day out so the luggers, to earn a bit extra cash, would take the overflow of people who wanted to go sharking.

To a drifter, sharks were nothing more than a damned menace because they would go for the pilchards caught in their nets and rip them to rags. To counteract this a shark line, made up from a few fathoms of buoy rope, light chain and a big hook, would be baited up and hung off the mizzen backstay while riding to the nets. When a shark took hold, it was hauled in hand over hand and dragged onto the boat. Its tail was cut off, and then it was thrown back again, to be seen last disappearing stern first, one less to rip the nets. A cruel way to kill them but the attitude was very different in those days.

When the luggers first started taking people out angling, it was looked upon as a way to exterminate as many sharks as possible (and there were a lot of them) while getting paid to do it. So away to sea they would go with twelve hapless anglers and, instead of the expected big game rod, they found themselves with a lugger's shark line.

The fun began when a shark took hold. The resulting contest was like something from the gladiatorial games of ancient Rome, man versus beast. An enraged fish, weighing anything up to a couple of hundred pounds or more on one end of a rope, and a terrified angler whose bowels were rapidly turning to water on the other. To lessen the angler's fright, and prevent the skin being torn off his hands by the rope or, worse still, being dragged overboard, the skipper would lend a hand.

While the contest was taking place, the other anglers would line the starboard rail, baying for the shark's blood in a bold and heroic manner ... that was, until the beast itself was boated by the skipper. Having been hauled aboard in fairly short order, the shark was far from exhausted and there it would lie, tail scything the air and beating the deck, rows of razor sharp teeth munching lumps out of the parting boards. On seeing this, the usual reaction from our heroic band of shark hunters was to stampede for the rear of the wheel-house in sheer jaw-dropping terror. Not until the skipper had subdued the shark by beating its head in with a big hammer would their bravado return.

This was not exactly a very sporting or safe way to take people out big game fishing, and after numerous complaints of rope-burnt hands and soiled underwear from the anglers, the committee of the Shark Angling Club of Great Britain called a meeting with the lugger skippers, chaired by its founder and president, Brigadier Caunter. In no uncertain terms it was 'requested' that in future, when out shark angling, they must use rods, and thereby uphold the safety and dignity of the sport. This was duly complied with, and the required rods were thereafter rented by the season from Jack Bray's tackle shop on East Looe quay.

Many years later there was a scheme running to attach a tag to the dorsal fin of sharks that were caught instead of killing them, recording the area and date of capture stamped on it. Released unharmed, the information they carried was used for further research. This shark-tagging scheme was a good thing and ran successfully for many years. Information about sharks caught off Looe came in from all around the Atlantic.

At one of the annual Shark Angling Club dinners, Brigadier Caunter (by then in his dotage) stood up to give his usual speech.

He rambled on for a while before dropping a real clanger: "And finally," he drawled, "I should like to thank the skippers for shagging the tarts!" The poor old boy inadvertently brought the house down, and I think it was the very last Angling Club dinner he ever attended.

Shark angling as a sport started in Looe quite by accident. In the late 1940s the brigadier, a keen big game angler, had originally chartered local angling boats to take him out to try and catch a tuna. These fish migrated in schools down Channel at certain times of the year and, although this particular fish always seemed to elude him, he did catch plenty of sharks. Returning to Looe with one or two of the larger ones on board, fishermen on the quay would pull his leg a bit. "A couple of nice tunny today then, Briggy," was a likely remark. Meanwhile, other anglers who had been out for the day doing battle with pollack and conger began to fancy a go themselves at this rather exciting new sport. Within a few years, shark angling became extremely popular, earning many thousands of pounds annually for the port.

During those busy holiday periods we could not have worked any harder and still remained alive. If the weather stayed workable, the boat's engines never went cold. We were out for five or six nights a week pilchard drifting, and every day with the shark anglers. Returning to harbour any time between three and six in the morning, the fish were landed and the boat scrubbed down. Then, instead of heading home to bed, the two men whose turn it was to go sharking would grab a bite to eat and maybe an hour in their bunks. At half past eight the boat was made ready, another quick scrub around (you could scrub for a week and still not get rid of all the fish scales) and the rods were passed up from the forepeak, ready to take out a dozen anglers at nine o'clock.

The sharking grounds were ten or twelve miles off the coast, and when we arrived, the day would be spent drifting broadside with the shark lines baited up and paid out on cork floats at varying distances from the boat, while a trail of 'rubby dubby' (mashed pilchards) was shaken from two mesh bags to attract the sharks. The best 'rubby' was salted down in a dustbin, making the fish soft and easy to shake out of the bags and also drawing the oil out of the fish, creating a much more effective trail to attract the sharks with. Its only drawback was the smell, an oily, all-pervading stench of

The lugger Iris *in the early 1920s, Looe, rigged for sail.*

*(L-R) Bruce 'Tiddler' Sammels, Clarence Libby, Roy Pengelly,
Frank 'Moogie' Pengelly on the* Iris *c1955*

The One Accord *in the 1950s: (L-R) Tommy Jolliff;
Lando Puckey; Edmund Curtis; Jack Jolliff.*

Hauling nets aboard the Iris *at night: 'Moogie', Harry Stevens and
Clarence Libby.*

Shaking out the nets at Looe quay, 1965

Net cart, c1910 (same one used in the 1960s). Charles Clausen holding the shafts, with James Toms, ? Prynn and Richard Pearce.

A big catch on the Iris, spring 1964.

Clarence Libby with the Looe ferry, c1965

Albert 'the Belgie' Daems, the Iris's 'scruffer'

The Undaunted, *first lugger in Looe to be fitted with an engine*

*Clarence Libby aboard the Iris,
making ready for a lining trip;
'Moogie' in the background*

The crew of the Looe lugger Iris, *1966. (L-R) Alfred 'Tiddler' Sammels; Harry 'Slender' Stevens; Paul Greenwood; Michael Pengelly; Frank 'Moogie' Pengelly; Jack Harris (foreground).*

Iris, *April 1965. End of the Channel lining season, the pilchards have arrived. Hauling the big summer fleet aboard.*

Iris coming into Looe (above)

The first motorised sailing luggers in Looe (below),
still carrying full sailing rig.

April 1965, at the end of the longline season. Hauling the main fleet aboard the Iris *to start the summer pilchard fishing*

Guide Me *entering Looe harbour with passengers*

The John Wesley *heading out of Looe*

Luggers off to the fishing ground, Looe

'Moogie' with first shark caught aboard the Iris.
Note shark handline on the aft deck.

Luggers putting to sea in the days of sail

The Iris *during a 'paint-up' in 1965.*
(L-R) Jack Moore; Harry Stevens; Paul Greenwood;
Alfred 'Tiddler' Sammels; Michael Pengelly; Frank 'Moogie' Pengelly

Channel lining aboard the Iris, *1968*

The Our Boys *making ready to enter harbour, 1960*

The Iris *during her last working days in the early 1970s.*
Eileen *and* Our Daddy *in the background.*

The Iris *in 1965 ('Skips' Ransome right, on quay)*

Our Boys *hand lining for mackerel, 1967*

The author aboard the Our Boys *with his wife Maggie.*

decaying fish. Many were the anglers who had their days entirely ruined by the lid of the 'rubby' bin being lifted prior to filling the bags. There was just no escaping the smell, and if the poor souls happened to be out on the *Our Boys* when Stan Mutton was in charge, they needed cast iron stomachs not to end up giving their breakfast a second viewing. Stan loved a salt pilchard snack and would select a couple for himself out of the bin; anyone feeling a bit cruddy but had managed to hold on so far despite the dreadful stench was surely done for as they watched in horror at somebody actually eating the stuff!

In those days it wasn't uncommon to catch ten, fifteen or even twenty sharks in a day, and there would be some fairly big beasts amongst them as well. Some of the older crews didn't want to bother with these, so while they were adjusting the clutch on the reel for the angler, a quick and unnoticed touch of a fag-end on the line would soon see the big ones on their way. A yellow flag was flown for every shark caught, and on some days the boats would be flying flags from the mizzen masthead to the stem head, extra flags being cut out from old oilskins.

Returning to Looe at six in the evening, the lugger was hitched up along side the quay to get the people ashore, then it was fish and chips and a mug of tea for dinner. The rest of the crew would be aboard by seven, and away we went for another night's pilchard drifting. A day's sharking meant an extra five pounds in the wage packet, but working 36 hour shifts, with sometimes very little rest in between, is not something I would want to do again. I often wonder what the visitors must have thought of it all when they stepped aboard for their day out. Two weary fishermen, stinking of pilchards and diesel, on a threadbare old boat, herself emitting a different but equally horrible smell from every hatch. It wasn't exactly five star treatment. Nevertheless curiosity got the better of some of them, because it was not at all unusual for one or two anglers from a sharking trip to come out for the night to see for themselves what pilchard drifting was all about, many of them taking photographs and cine film. Some even volunteered their services on the nets. To this end they would be dressed up in old oilskins and sea boots and be put 'out the rail'. Ten minutes was about as long as any of them lasted, the dip net suited them much the best. One lad I remember was as keen as mustard with this tool. 'Tiddler' had lifted up the head ropes so as he could get in closer to the fish dropping away from a small meshed net then being hauled. With about three stone in the dip net, the lad launched the long handle back inboard prior to lifting it aboard and in doing so, caught 'Tiddler' right in the bread basket, knocking him down into the net room where he lay winded, like a turtle on it's back. The rest of us couldn't do a thing to help him as we were all crippled with laughing. Luckily we were nearly all in with the catch and he didn't have far to fall; the only thing bruised was his dignity

If the weather stayed fine for any length of time, we ended up like the walking dead. What a relief it could be to see the gale cone hoisted on the coastguard flagstaff. But every possible pound had to be earned in the summer, because in the winter the dole and a few odd jobs had been the way of things for many years.

The golden rule aboard the boats then, as now, was no drinking at sea. Several men might turn up to go to sea having had a few jars, but there was no more to be had on the boats, and they soon sobered up. Every boat carried a bottle of whisky, but this was purely for medicinal use only. However, there was one area of operation where this rule could not very well be applied, and that was when out sharking. Many of the anglers loved to take a drop of booze with them on their big day out, and some of the old skippers just couldn't turn down a quick gargle if it was on offer. There were a few incidents where it went a bit further than a gargle, but all in all, most of them managed to hold out, at least until they got ashore into the pub. There they could play the old seadog-skipper role for all it was worth, while their admiring audience plied them into near oblivion with free beer.

But those men were great characters, and their like does not exist today. They could tell of the days when they were boys, crewing on the schooners and ketches that traded around the coast under sail, and as young men working on the big J class racing yachts; of service in the Royal Navy during the war, and of fishing seasons when money was plentiful, and times when they nearly starved. They have all gone now, and the port is very much the poorer for their passing.

8

Barking the Nets

The drift nets we used were made of fine cotton twine and required an awful lot of looking after. There was always mending to be done where sharks had torn into them, or when they had fouled up while shooting or hauling in poor weather. To prevent them from going rotten, the nets that were being worked had to be treated with a preservative every six weeks or so.

There were two methods of doing this; the newest nets were 'barked', while the older ones were 'pickled'. Neither job was pleasant, but pickling was by far the worst of the two. On the day the skipper arranged to bark the nets we would try to get in early from sea, land the catch and then drop the boat back at the bark house. The nets would then be hauled ashore and built up like a haystack outside the bark house door. Buoys and buffs were cast off and stowed on the foredeck. By then Frank Hoskin, who owned the bark house, would have the boiler lit, building up a good head of steam. In front of the boiler was a brick-lined pit about four feet square by three feet deep which was two-thirds filled with water. Steam pipes would get this pit bubbling hot, and into it the cracked up bark or 'kutch' would be dissolved. This stuff was processed from the bark of a tropical tree and packed in half hundred weight sacks, it resembled dark, dirty-looking amber.

A roller was shipped up at the bark house door and, at a slow and steady pace, two men hauled the nets in, dropping them fathom by fathom into the pit. The skipper stood by with a pole, poking everything well down to make sure it all got a good soaking as well as regulating the speed to make sure that the bark didn't go off the boil. With his hands protected by a pair of heavy rubber gloves, a fourth man pulled the nets out again, and behind him two more of the crew, one on the head ropes, one on the skirt, stowed them neatly by the exit hatch on the sloping floor to drain. Last of all the mizzen sail and the mooring ropes were dumped into the pit to have a soak. The whole process took about three hours. It was like working in very hot fog and we would nearly melt into our boots.

The nets were then left to drain for a few hours before being hauled back aboard. The fleet would now be down in the net-room back to front, so we had to shoot head to wind and change ends to put it right. This was important, because the newest nets were always the ones nearest to the boat and therefore likely to suffer least damage. The ones furthest away towards the 'pole end' were the longest in the water and much more likely to suffer shark damage, or be cut up by a coaster going over them. In fact the last couple of nets of the fleet or 'pole-enders' were very often rotten ripe, hanging away in rags off the head ropes, but they always seemed to fish very well in that condition.

Every time a net was barked the heat of the process shrank the mesh a little, so after a few years an alternative method of preservation had to be used to stop them from becoming useless. This method was called 'pickling', a process that every one hated, but there was no alternative. Harry and I used to get nabbed for this - the boy and the cook - the two least likely to have some other pressing job or be able to talk our way out of it. The nets needing this treatment were piled onto the net cart (an old wooden-wheeled donkey cart) and the two of us would drag it off to the pickling store, a tiny stone built shed in the back streets. Inside this place was an old domestic bath half full of water with a huge draining board attached to one end of it, and on top of the water floated about 20 gallons of creosote.

Wearing oilskin aprons and plastic gloves for protection, I would pull the nets off the cart and into the bath and Harry then dragged them through the creosote and stacked them on the draining board, a filthy job. The nets were then left to drain for a couple of days before being hauled aboard the boat, and until the stuff worked out of them a bit, they were dreadful to handle. Creosote burned your face and stung your eyes, you were black up to the elbows, and your oilskin was covered in it but, as Jack used to say, "If you can't take a joke you shouldn't have joined".

There was a day when Harry failed see the funny side. He and

I had dragged a cartload of nets down to the store and were well into the routine of this horrible task when Harry suddenly needed to pump ship so, pulling off his gloves, he nipped outside to relieve himself. Suddenly a howl went up: he had somehow got a dollop of creosote on the end of his 'old man' and, with eyes a-water and burning member in hand, he dashed to his cottage to gain some relief. His speed on the straight was very impressive, and I don't think anyone wearing hobnail boots has ever cornered so fast; the sparks fairly flew, it was as if he was going down the road full throttle on an invisible motorbike. I know it sounds cruel, but I now know exactly what people mean when they say they nearly died laughing.

As the fishing season progressed, so the size of the pilchards changed and to match this, small or big meshed nets were being hauled in or out of the boat all the time. When nets were finished with for the season, they were put onto the cart and hauled up to the net spars, there to be hung up in the wind to dry before being stowed up the loft. If they were put away wet, or even damp, they would heat up and rot just like a compost heap. There was even a danger of spontaneous combustion. For this same reason, if we were weather bound for more than three days, the fleet of nets had to be hauled up out of the net room and stacked on deck to cool and air it, then hauled back down again three days later, the process repeated until the weather improved. If the fishing had been heavy, the nets would be soaked in pilchard oil and full of scales, heads and quite a few whole fish. This would really speed the heating up process, making the nets nearly too hot to handle. Towards the middle of the fleet there would be a steaming miasma of rotting fish billowing out over the hatch coamings, a good lungful of which could send you retching to the rail.

Another danger to the nets was rats. The rich oily smell of pilchards would attract them aboard the boats in search of a meal. Inevitably they would end up in the net room, burrowing from morsel to morsel through the nets. Then the next time the fleet was shot there would be dozens of rat-sized holes, entailing hours of work with the net needles to repair. The answer to the problem was 'Scamp', Moogie's Jack Russell terrier. Put aboard a boat and given the magic word "rats", he would go into action like a canine version of the avenging angel. After a sniff about to get the scent, he was off snuffling and yapping, with the crew stood by to shift anything that might be standing between him and his victim. Coils of rope, fish boxes, fenders and boards were all cast aside for this small dog, who was worked up into a pitch of fury by all about him shouting "Rats, Scamp, rats!" and "Where is he? Tear the bastard to shreds!" etc. Suddenly he would make a lunge, there would be a terrified squeal from the rat and Scamp would appear with it in his jaws to the cheers and praise of the boat's crew and any others who had gathered around to watch the fun. I don't think I have ever seen a dog looking so completely and utterly pleased with itself at that moment.

9

Herring Fishing

Our sharking season ended with the school summer holidays. It was a nice extra in the wages, but we were all glad when it was over. With autumn approaching, it wouldn't be many weeks before the pilchard season also ground to a halt. The boats would chase the migrating shoals up and down the coast for ever-diminishing catches, and by November they would be gone. From then on there was very little to be earned fishing until the following March when, hopefully, enough pilchards could be caught to bait up the long lines.

After a hard summer season the autumn fishing was very pleasant. Because the sun was setting much earlier, we would leave the harbour just after lunch. Shooting the nets at teatime, we would be hauling by about seven o'clock and very often be back in the harbour again by midnight, sometimes even earlier. If we were working close to home and Neptune had decided not to let us have any of his fish that night, 'Tiddler', back on the head ropes, might take a look at the wheel-house clock, do a quick calculation and then announce that if we got our fingers out we could save tide in for a pint. If that idea took hold then look out: we went from jogging along steadily on an easy haul, to working as if the Devil himself was after us. The pawl on the roller would go from a steady click, click, to one continuous clatter. Clearing the nets out, water and fish would be flying everywhere, and the old engine was in gear more than it was out, driving the boat along the fleet. Arriving back into harbour with maybe only minutes to spare before closing time, everything was done for speed. Ropes and fenders were put out, the leg shipped, boxes of fish thrown up on the quay to be weighed. 'Moogie', who wasn't a drinking man, would be shaking his head and saying, "If only you bastards could work like this normally, we would all be rich," as he watched his crew rip off their oilskins and stampede for the pub.

71

Although the wages were tailing off rapidly, it was easy work, and we were usually home for the best part of a night's kip. The married men would joke about getting home 'under the lee of bum island' and if they were lucky, 'catching it with the dew on'.

At that time I had somehow been given the job of boat's fish jowter, so when we returned home with only a small catch of mixed fish, herrings, mackerel and pilchards, it was my job to sell them. By nine o'clock I would be back aboard the boat to lift up the hatches and drag out the boxes of fish that represented our night's work. Loading them onto the net cart, I would go to my pitch under the arch in Fore Street, and sell them at 6d a fish. Stan Mutton off the *Our Boys* had a pitch by the town clock. Whatever I made was always shared out as stocker, i.e. divided equally among the crew, but no share for the boat. It was very often cold and draughty standing in that alleyway flogging fish, but luckily an ancient retired butcher by the name of Dick Wickett, (known to the local lads as 'Old Dick Fuckit') lived in a cottage nearby and he used to bring me a mug of cocoa and a sandwich in exchange for a couple of herrings.

By late October 1964, the fishing had dwindled away to nothing and the luggers had hauled their nets ashore to begin the long winter's lay up. But rather than do nothing, our skipper, along with Bill 'Pye' Pengelly and his crew on the *Our Boys* decided to haul a fleet of herring nets aboard and work out of Brixham, trying our luck on the 'silver darlings' around Torbay. For generations the Cornish luggers had gone to Brixham in October to fish the herring shoals that came in to spawn in the big sandy bays, but that was now only a memory. The ministry of 'Ag and Fish' still paid a small trip subsidy to herring drifters, so if we only caught one herring to prove we had been to sea, the subsidy was paid, which meant at the very least the boat would not go into debt. It was better to try and earn something than tie up with a certainty of earning nothing.

So, on a fine Sunday morning in late October, with ten herring nets stowed in the net room and a few baskets of line on deck, we headed for Torbay in the company of the *Our Boys*. As we would be living on the boat, each of the crew had a bag of spare clothes and washing kit. When fishing away, the skipper provided bread and jam and a big slab cake, and each evening a meal of some description was scraped together. Anything else, you got it yourself. It was a fine run up the coast, catching the flood tide around Start Point and arriving in Torbay during the late afternoon. The two boats scouted around for any sign of herring as well as keeping a lookout for the *Bluebell*, owned by the Fry brothers, and the *Hopeful*, skippered by Peter Easton. They were two little inshore boats that also fished for herring, working moored nets around the bay, and we didn't want to get afoul of them as we would be working right in the shallow waters. Because of this, the buoy ropes had been shortened up from three fathoms to one; sometimes we would be so close to the shore that the buoys had to be flung in under the head ropes, and still the nets would touch the sand. We had to be careful when hauling because of weaver fish, tin cans and 'gooseberry bushes' - spiky little bushes that got tangled up in the nets, though what they really were and where they came from I have no idea.

A likely area in the bay was selected and the nets were shot. Then, after a quick scrub around, the spars were shipped up and we all went below for a helping of stew that Harry had cooked for our supper. He had made enough to last us for two days and kept the big dixie lashed to the engine to make it quicker to warm up the next day. Working a short fleet of nets in shallow water didn't take much time or effort to haul, so we would usually shoot three times a night. The only disadvantage was for the man out the rail where, instead of laying back and hauling the nets over the roller, he had to stand tight out to the rail and lift them over because herrings didn't hit into the net very hard. They seemed only to poke their noses into the mesh and then give up. To us this was very easy work; instead of picking, twisting and thrashing the nets to get pilchards out, all the herrings required was a little flap and out they fell, lovely plump glittering fish, slithering down the deck.

After a night of shooting and hauling around Torbay, we went into Brixham to land in time for the fish auction. Mooring up in the inner harbour, we then carried the few stone of herring that we had caught, up to the market in maund baskets. It had been a long day and night. The *Our Boys* tied up along side us and we helped to put her catch ashore. Afterwards it was smocks and overalls off and climb into our bunks for a few hours kip until lunchtime. Then those who liked their beer went ashore for a few pints, while others had fish and chips and a stroll around the harbour, followed by a couple more hours in the bunk before it was time to go to sea again. Dinner would be dished out while riding to the nets on the first shoot of the night. A couple of times a week it would be Harry's famous stew, at other times baked herring was dish of the day or, if someone had scrounged around the trawlers, we might have a boiled plaice or a bun crab each, all bulked out with plenty of bread and butter. 'Afters' was a slab of cake and a mug of tea to complete the meal.

I once made the mistake of asking Harry what we were going to have for dinner that night. "I'll boil up a Feenock," came the answer, and of course I fell for it. "What's a Feenock?" I asked, right on cue. "A donkey's cock stuffed with onions," came our cook's reply, grinning from ear to ear, tickled to bits by his own wit. Another dish we were always threatened with was 'half a leg of a sheep's head'. Having been a baker for many years Harry had one golden rule: when it's brown it's done, and when it's black it's buggered. TV chefs, eat your hearts out.

If the wind was blowing too hard to go to sea, we would all have a wash and brush up before going ashore to either the pub or the cinema. A deck bucket full of fresh water was heated up on the stove, and then placed on the cabin sole where we could all sit around it. First it was out soap and flannels and we all had a wash. Then everyone lathered up and the razors were employed. Lastly, with a drop of water poured into our tea mugs from the kettle, teeth were cleaned (false or otherwise) with everyone spitting into the wash bucket. When the ablutions were completed, Harry would take that same bucket of water and scrub out the cabin.

There were no toilet facilities of any kind on the luggers. If you needed a pee, you did it over the rail; the other call of nature was dealt with in the same manner. Perched on the rail with your bare arse hanging over the water, shirt tail flapping in the breeze, you clung to the mizzen backstay with one hand, a sheet of newspaper in the other, and a far away look in the eye. If it was very cold or rough, a drop of seawater was dipped up in a deck bucket and you retired with it down forward. 'Tiddler', our champion beer drinker, used to really suffer, sometimes having to hang off the backstay several times a night as he didn't dare pass wind in his trousers for fear of an accident.

When going for a run ashore, smocks and overalls were taken off, and a coat or jacket was worn instead. But working and sleeping in the same clothes all week meant the smell of fish, diesel and BO must have been fairly overpowering and although nobody in the pubs seemed to mind, we could clear a fair area around us when we went to the cinema.

Going to the cinema was a farce. I don't think anyone ever managed to watch a film right through. Because we worked by day and by night, in fact anytime at all, the wheels and springs of our body clocks were scattered far and wide, and we became adjusted to snatching an hour or so whenever we could. Being warm, dark and comfortable, the cinema was the ideal place for a kip and it wouldn't be long before we all started nodding off. Every now and then you would come to and try and work out what the film was all about, glancing around to see who else was awake. But after ten minutes or so the heavy eyelids would get the better of you and off you went again. It was only the stampede of the rest of the audience trying to get out before 'God Save The Queen' was played that roused us to make our own exit.

The last fishing night of the week was Friday, and after landing our catch on Saturday morning, we would then go home for the weekend. 'Skips' Ransom, a retired RAF officer living in Looe, drove us back and forth in his car, a big black Humber Hawk, while Freddie Lewis, a Looe boatman, chauffeured the crew of the *Our Boys* in his Bedford van.

'Moogie' always sat in the front with Skips, while the rest of us bunched up in the back. Our skipper had never driven a car in his life, but on this particular morning he was being rather observant. Suddenly he pipes up, "Here, Skips," he says. "There doesn't seem to be a hell of a lot of difference between steering a boat and driving a car. You've got a wheel for hard to port and hard to starboard and a lever for ahead and astern." "Well maybe you'll have to have a go one day," said Skips. "Fucked if I won't," said Moogie. It was probably fortunate for us all that he never did.

Upon our return to Brixham on Monday afternoon we would climb down aboard the old *Iris*, pump her out and make ready for sea. Then another week of shooting and hauling the herring nets around Torbay would begin. Thus we passed the time until the two luggers were steamed back to Looe for the Christmas break. We didn't catch a lot of herring, but the little money we did make, combined with the subsidy and a bit of dole money for bad weather days, made us a wage of sorts, five or six pounds a week, maybe ten if we had been lucky. It kept the wolf from the door, but only just.

10

April Gales

The intention had been to return to Brixham after Christmas, but the weather took a turn for the worst, completely wiping out January and February. The herring nets were hauled ashore, dried and stowed back up the loft. I managed to get a few weeks' work labouring for a builder, Jack worked on a coal round, while 'Moogie', 'Tiddler' and Harry passed the time up in the loft overhauling nets and lines.

By mid March the weather was settling down a bit, so the skipper decided we should haul in a short bait fleet of nets and put the lines aboard. But, as the saying goes, 'Everything in our favour was against us'. When the weather was right, we couldn't catch enough pilchards for a bait up. When we caught some bait, the weather was too poor to go out in the Channel, so the lines were shot along the shore for black conger. These sold for next to nothing per stone because much of the catch was small stuff known as 'arse worms'. After a winter spent scratching about, everyone was desperate to get some money coming in. We were all skint.

One night in early April we found ourselves with plenty of bait, but yet again the weather was shaping up to be pretty grim. 'Moogie' could stand it no longer, however, so away out in the Channel we had to go, 'shit or bust'. Harry cut the pilchards up while the rest of us were on our knees beside the baskets of line, baiting the hooks with pieces of fish taken from a washing up bowl resting on top of the line. Hook held in the right hand, a piece of bait in the lef t, to be hooked through twice, heads down, tails up, all hanging down neatly from the rim of the basket. Four baskets of line per man, 250 hooks per basket, unless you had a box, and that could contain up to 400 hooks.

Before we were many miles out, the wind and sea started to make down Channel, and by the time we reached the lining grounds 40 miles out it was certainly poor enough. But the lines were all baited up, so they had to be shot. The old *Iris* was squared away before wind and tide, then shooting commenced. Over went the first dann, with its black flags and two hurricane lamps, then the dann line, ending with a grape anchor to which the end of the first basket of line was tied. 'Tiddler' was at the wheel, keeping her on course, with 'Moogie' shooting the line, right arm swinging as he threw the seven miles of rope away tight and straight. Clarence stood behind him with a sharp knife to cut any hooks away should they catch up on the boat or shooter. He was also ready to knock the engine in and out of gear, to 'Moogie's orders.

Jack, Harry and I dragged the baskets of line to the shooting platform at the aft end of the starboard waterways, to bend the end of the basket of line then being shot to the top of the next one. Then pull the empty basket away and lift the next one up in place, and so on, to make one 'long line'. The middle dann line, with its brick sinker, was bent on with a rolling hitch and shot away from the port quarter, followed by its dann. Hooks were now flying over the side at a great rate, engine in gear in the troughs, and out when we surge ahead on a sea. Seven miles later, away went the end of the last basket of line, with its anchor and dann line, followed by the boat dann, hurricane lamps flickering, big black flags crackling in the wind.

Down went the wheel and as we came up head to wind, the mizzen was hoisted and sheeted home; the skipper took the wheel and proceeded to stay in sight of the dann for the next couple of hours until the tide turned and the haul could begin. Empty line baskets were stacked and lashed and anything that might move was secured - it was now time for a mug of tea and a bite to eat. The wind was freshening up all the time and by now some really big lumps of sea were starting to build. Moogie kept the old boat riding head to wind; thankfully she didn't make hard work of it.

At slack water the jinny was started, the dann was gaffed aboard and we went to work, the seas by now big and breaking. Regardless, the old jinny chuffed away, the skipper was hauling behind it, and the line was steadily coming aboard. 'Tiddler' was coiling, Jack was gaffing, I was unhooking the fish, while Harry worked the wheel and engine. Clarence was waiting for the first length of line to come aboard to start repairing and clearing it back into the baskets. I don't remember how much line we had hauled, two or three baskets at the most, when suddenly a huge sea reared up, the boat pointed her bow at the sky and surfed away stern first, and the line parted. Here was a problem. To haul the rest of the line, we would have to battle our way up to the other dann and ride around until the tide turned again. The skipper looked around at the weather and, as tough as he was, he knew when he was beaten.

"That will do, boys, we're going home," was his decision. He stopped the jinny and strode back to the wheelhouse. Labouring head to wind, anything and everything that might move or be washed about was secured, including the hatches which were spiked down with nails. When all was ready, we stowed the mizzen and 'Moogie' awaited his moment to bring us around on a course for home without the seas sweeping the deck. Once safely around, the two forward engines were cranked into life, then the forehatch was spiked down as well.

There was now nothing more to be done, so we retired below, shipped up the weather- boards and slid the hatch shut to prevent gallons of seawater cascading down the companionway ladder. We climbed into our bunks, but there was precious little rest to be had in them. The *Iris* was rearing and plunging so much, that no matter how you tried to brace yourself, you were still flung about. Being thrown about down the cabin like that was dreadful for seasickness, especially with the hatch shut tight building up heat and fumes from the range and the engine. I know for sure that I wasn't the only one to throw up on that trip home.

Every so often 'Tiddler' would lift a board in the cabin sole and peer down into the bilge to see how much water she was making. Then, with the shout of, "Whose turn is it?" one of us would have to dress up in sea boots, oilskins, sou'wester and muffler to go up on deck to pump out. One blessing was that the pump didn't need priming, the deck was awash and the air full of flying spray. Braced against the bucking and plunging of the boat, you swung away at the pump, stopping every now and then to hang on tight to the mizzen jump stay as a big cresting sea made her lurch violently, causing the props to race and thrash up foam. Eventually the pump would suck dry and then, thankfully, you could slip back down the cabin to your bunk, knowing four others had to go through it before it was your turn again.

How long it took to get back to Looe, I can't remember, but I do know we were all very glad to arrive. It had been a hard, wet, miserable trip, we hadn't caught any fish and to add insult to injury, the weather had driven us back into the harbour, leaving most of the gear still out in the Channel.

Three days later, the sun was shining and the sea was sparkling calm, so away we went again to see if we could retrieve the line. This was long before anyone had Decca or GPS. The only navigation aids a skipper had were a clock to tell him how long he had run for, a compass to steer a course by and a tide book to work out the tidal flow. 'Moogie' had set the course and timed the run out, then he started to box the area. Down to the west for so long, then turn, out a bit and up to the east again. We boxed around like this for several hours and had no joy whatsoever, all eyes straining until we were seeing danns everywhere. The skipper had almost given up hope, but decided on one more run before we turned for home.

Thinking that would be it, I nipped down the cabin and put a steak and kidney pie in the oven for dinner. It was on that last run, pushing a bit further to the east, that the shout went up, "There it is!" and away in the distance we could all now make out the black flags of the pole end dann, 40 miles out in the Channel. All was made ready and when we arrived at the dann, it was gaffed aboard. With everyone at their stations, the haul began.

Unlike the last time we had been out there, the weather was perfect and, with the old jinny on full throttle, the line fairly flew aboard, arm over arm. All the gear was retrieved, but we didn't have much of a catch of fish, just a few stone of poor looking ray and conger (they had been on the hooks far too long); any other fish had either worked their way off or had been eaten by their mates. By the time the end of the gear flipped over the jinny wheel, my forgotten pie was a charred ruin. But, not to worry, a mug of tea and a bite to eat was enjoyed before we set to work again, clearing and repairing the lines back into the baskets as we steamed back home to Looe.

As an old man, 30 plus years later, 'Moogie' still talked about that trip. He had experienced many hard times, but I think that one stood out in his memory.

11

The Engines

Between the ending of the lining season in early May and the start of the summer pilchard drifting, the *Iris* was treated to her annual paint up. This wasn't a very elaborate affair. She was taken over to West Looe where she would dry out at low water. When the tide had ebbed enough for us to wade about in our sea-boots, all hands would set to with deck scrubbers working the tide down to clean the weed and barnacles off the boat's bottom. Then at low water, with the sun and wind drying the planking, cans of anti fouling, or 'patent' as it was called, were stirred up and lapped on with 'long tom' brushes. Black bitumastic paint was slapped on the sides and outside bulwarks. The inside bulwarks were painted white, while hatches, coamings and covering boards were painted blue after a quick rattle about with some blunt scrapers. For quickness the paint was a mixture of half undercoat and half gloss. The last thing to be painted was the deck, for which all the leftover paint was tipped into a deck bucket and stirred up, then paraffin added to bulk it out. On some paint ups, the wheelhouse would get a coat of its own brown and cream, but as for down below, I never saw that painted at all. I think fish oil, diesel and smoke preserved her below decks. The skipper used to take great care cutting in the name and fishing numbers on the luff of each bow. I can see him now, balancing on the top of a set of steps, brush in hand, making faces fit to win a girning contest in his concentration to get it neat. If the weather was kind to us the whole job would be completed in just two days, then it was back to East Looe to haul the fleet of nets aboard to begin the summer season.

The 1965 season started bleak, and continued to be so. There were plenty of pilchards and because of this, the cannery tried to reduce the price paid per stone to the boats from 3/6d (17p) to 3/- (15p), so we all went on strike. After three nights ashore, they relented and agreed to pay 3/6d again; considering they were paying 4/6d per stone 20 years before, we weren't exactly being overpaid.

No sooner was this business settled than the main engine, the 45 HP in the cabin, died on us. It had been running very badly for months, with the exhaust stack above deck glowing red hot in the dark, leaving a trail of sparks and flame behind us. Because of this, Frankie Oliver on the *Our Daddy* nicknamed her 'the old black dragon'. We were a fortnight ashore while the engine was being repaired, but it wasn't all bad - I had two weeks blow out on sleep and attended plenty of parties and barbeques, a welcome change from hard labour.

The forward engine room was the home of the 30 and the 21 HP Listers. It was entered via a small deck hatch at the luff of the port bow, a four-rung ladder took you down into it, the only place below decks with near-standing headroom. An ordinary domestic switch operated the lights which consisted of two small bulbs dangling from the deck head by their wires. Aft from the ladder were the two dark green painted engines with their open fly wheels and belts. These engines were dry sump, so beside each a brass five gallon tank piped lubricating oil to them, while fuel was gravity fed from a couple of 30 gallon tanks under the deck head to port and starboard, secured on stout wooden beds.

Right in the forepeak was the cable tier, a heavy plank shelf supported by battens fastened to the port and starboard frames, about two feet down from the deck head and extending back from the stem five feet or so. Here, lashed down hard and fast was the anchor and its tarred cable.

The engine room had once been painted grey or white, but the overall colour was now black from the smeech of the engines. Occasionally somebody was sent down there with a deck broom and a bucket of diesel to give it a scrub out - another choice job. The deck head had never been painted and from it, foot-long fronds of black pluffy wood used to dangled down, brushing your hat as you moved about. These fronds were caused by sea water soaking through the deck over the years and being crystallised by the heat of the engines, the expanding salt pushing the wood fibres apart, then to hang down like soggy rope ends. To cure this problem we nailed strips of hardboard up over the worst areas.

One summer the exhaust pipe on the '30' cracked and, as the weather was fine, the boat continued working 24 hours a day so there was no time to fix it until the weather turned. Meantime, to stop the forward engines the hatch was first lifted to allow billows of hot brown exhaust smoke to escape, then down the ladder you went, taking a deep breath of fresh air that hopefully would last you until you emerged again. It was like descending into a small compact version of hell: you couldn't see anything, the noise of the engine was deafening, there was nothing to breath and the heat had the sweat pouring off you in seconds. Groping through the oven hot blackness, the throttles were first eased back then the engines were knocked out of gear, next the engine stop levers were held back allowing the fly wheels to slow to a leisurely halt. By that time you were turning purple and spluttering on the fumes, going for the hatch and fresh air as if your life depended on it, which I suppose it did. We were more than pleased when that exhaust was eventually repaired. There were no fire extinguishers, sprinkler systems or safety equipment of any kind in the engine room, only an assortment of ancient spanners kept in a wooden box lodged behind the ladder which, because of its location, was usually full of water.

The '45', being the newest and most-used engine, was treated to five gallons of new oil every year; the '30' got the old oil from the '45', while the poor old '21' had to make do with the two-year old stuff from the '30'. Getting rid of the stinking dregs from the '21' was not a problem, it was simply drained straight down into the bilge.

By the season of 1967 the '21' needed so much 'easy start' to get it going that the two men winding the handle were nearly rendered unconscious. Eventually it was abandoned on its bed, never to run again. With the 45 HP Lister back in good running order it was back to business. The fleet had been catching plenty of fish, not only in Looe but in Mevagissey and Newlyn. This was more than the cannery could handle, so we were put on a limit of 120 stone per boat. Unfortunately, you can't regulate how much fish goes into a drift net; you can shorten up the number of nets you work, shoot, then haul more or less straight away, but when the pilchard shoals are running you are going to catch them. And so we did, coming into harbour with the decks loaded, scooping up 25 five stone cans for the lorry, then shovelling the rest over the side. It was a heartbreaking and wasteful thing to have to do. The five

Looe drifters carpeted the bottom of the harbour with unwanted pilchards, slocking in hundreds of bass and mullet for a free meal.

Coming in from sea one morning in late October, we landed the catch and the last drums of diesel were tipped in the fuel tanks. It was time for a refill. We were working out the last of the pilchard season, the wind had been south-westerly for several days, not blowing hard enough to keep us in from sea, but enough to make life wet and uncomfortable and never able to get out of our oilskins. All the rest of the empty drums were brought out from the store and loaded on deck, and Jack Harris and I were the lucky pair to go with the skipper on the run to Plymouth.

Diesel in those days was 1/3d (7p) a gallon and the local marine engineer, Ken Newton, and his son Robert would bring it to the boats in five gallon drums on their hand cart. However, the depot at Plymouth sold it for 1/- (5p) per gallon for a minimum order of 300 gallons, so 'Moogie' had 60 or more five gallon drums kept in a ground level store, and when they were empty all hands would load up the *Iris*'s decks and he and a couple of the crew would steam to Plymouth for a refill. The amazing thing about these drums was that originally they had held treacle, and great dollops of the stuff used to fall into the funnel when we were pouring fuel, but this extra in their diet never seemed to worry the engines.

We rolled away up to Plymouth Sound in a lumpy sea and drizzle rain, made fast along side the jetty in the Cattewater where a big hose was passed down and fuelling up began. Filling five-gallon drums from a hose designed to refuel coasters was a ticklish task, but eventually the last drum was topped up and we were on our way for home. Bashing around Penlee Point the old *Iris* was throwing back the spray and Jack and I were sheltering behind the wheelhouse with a mug of tea in our hands when suddenly I remembered the date. "It's my birthday today," I mentioned to Jack. "How old now then?" he asked. "Seventeen," I said. "Happy birthday," was the reply, and we chinked our tea mugs together.

Arriving back in Looe, all hands stowed the diesel drums back into the store, and away we went again for another wet rolly night at sea. Happy birthday indeed.

12

Working Big Shoals

A big shoal (or 'scull' as it was called) of pilchards would give its presence away no matter how deep it was swimming. The first sign looked for was the black water: whether the fish turned the water black themselves, or the plankton they fed on had that effect, I don't know, but either way pilchard water looked as black as pitch. The next sign would be very fine, light hints of fish oil coming to the surface from the underlying shoal. Downwind we could smell it from a fair distance away. Feeding off this oil would be the stormy petrels, 'Mother Carey's chickens' was the fishermen's name for them. These little birds looked like swallows with tiny hooked beaks and webbed feet, flying low over the surface of the sea, tiny feet tip-tipping the water, their heads bobbing up and down dipping up droplets of fish oil. Keeping them company would be the guillemots, scattered around above the shoals in twos and threes. These sharp-beaked, black-brown birds about the size of a small duck are the champion deep divers of the sea bird world, able to swim down as deep as 30 or 40 fathoms to feed off a shoal of fish.

If there were no sharks, whales or dolphins harassing the shoal, then the fish would stay down deep, it being too dangerous for them to come near the surface in daylight. The drifters would shoot their nets above these deep laying shoals and as darkness crept into the water so the fish would rise up under the safety of its cover to feed on the plankton, (their natural predators can't see to operate at night), only to run into miles of drift nets laying in wait.

If a large shoal of fish was being harassed by something a little more serious than guillemots and Mother Carey's chickens, then we would witness the most amazing drama. When the big predators go into action they drive the fish up towards the surface, and as soon as they rise to within reach of the gannets and gulls, a feeding frenzy of near unbelievable noise and magnitude takes place. Gannets, so numerous that you just couldn't begin to guess at their numbers, circle up in the sky over the fish, then suddenly go into a vertical crash dive, wings folded, powering into the sea like aquatic fighter planes. They utter a deep harsh quack, quack, quack noise just before hitting the water, making a crisp thudding sound when they do so. Thirty or 40 feet is about as deep as they go before bursting back up to the surface with more harsh quacking, flapping vigorously up into the air, rapidly gaining altitude to repeat the process. It's truly baffling how the hundreds diving down don't get tangled up with those climbing back up and how those circling above pick their moment to dive. They display a degree of precision and skill that makes the best human aviators look utterly ham-fisted.

Add to this, myriads of herring gulls screaming, squawking, fighting and scrounging for anything they can get hold of, regardless of who caught it first. Any bird with a fish in its beak gets unmercifully mobbed until it either swallows it, or is robbed. Gulls can't dive, but they do try if the fish are driven right to the surface. From a height of 40 feet or so they fold one wing and hurtle down broadside at the water, hitting it with a splash, instantly bobbing to the surface again, having gone down all of six inches. A useless pursuit, at the wrong angle and depth, but they must think it will come good one day. While all this mayhem is going on the real pirate of the air, the skua, (or the 'Tom Harry Shit Bird' as it's known in Looe) is swooping about awaiting its chance. The 'Tom Harry' is about the size of a gull, but leaner, meaner and much more streamlined with brown-black plumage. They live on fish but never catch any of their own. Instead they wait for a gull with a full crop to take to the air, they then chivvy and panic their victim until it throws up its catch in order to escape this unwanted attention. With the gull's dinner now plunging seaward, the 'Tom Harry' crash dives to catch his ill gotten gains in mid air, as smart and as neat as can be. A bastard of a bird but you have got to admire them.

The drifters from Looe and the luggers *Erin*, *Lindy Lou* and *Snowdrop* from Mevagissey would be motoring about with their echo sounders operating, trying to get an idea of how extensive the shoal was and in which direction it was moving. All the while, the squawking and screaming of thousands of over-excited seabirds is nearly enough to drive you insane, you feel as if your brain is going to come loose on its holding bolts. But as the sun drops low and the light gradually goes out of the water, the daytime predators pack up and all goes quiet once more. We are the night watch, it's our turn to have a go now. "God speed the plough," says 'Moogie' as the pole end buoy goes over the side, then we're off downwind with the buoys and buffs splashing overboard, the shooting roller chattering away to itself. We shan't ride to the gear for too long tonight; we could be in for a hard haul.

Heavy fishing meant hours of hauling and dragging which, in turn, led to sea-boils and poisoned hands. The sleeves of your oilskins would chafe your wrists raw, rubbing in all sorts of muck as it did so. Pretty soon you would end up with a ring of yellow-headed sea-boils each about a quarter of an inch across, and they stung like hell. To relieve the pain you rolled your oilskin sleeves up a bit to get clear of them, then a second ring would appear and again you would roll your sleeves up to a third position. By the time boils appeared there, the first lot had healed a bit so down went the sleeves, and it started all over again. After hauling for an hour or so the pain wore off a fair bit, and so if you didn't look you wouldn't notice that your oilskin sleeve was chafing them to a patch of raw flesh which was bleeding steadily. When your wrists got really horrible, bandages were tried, but wet bandages don't stay in place for very long. The forearms of a drifter-man were always a mass of sea-boil scars.

Because you were twisting and flipping fish out of the nets all the time, your fingers and palms of the hand went black from hundreds of tiny fish bones embedded in the skin. The short fine bones were no problem, it was the longer ones piercing into the flesh that caused the trouble. The end result was puss-swollen fingers and the backs of the hands red and puffy. Saturday was poisoned-finger day; you sharpened your penknife and squeezed the offending digit to find where the poison lay closest to the skin, then lanced it. If you couldn't face doing it yourself, you got somebody else to lance it while you looked away.

But the fish that really tore our hands to ribbons were scads (horse mackerel), totally armoured up with razor sharp spikes and prickles. After picking a yaffle of them out of the nets it was agony to even catch hold of the mooring ropes to tie the boat up in the harbour.

Some men really suffered, getting a red line up their arm and a lump under the armpit. When that happened it was time to see the doctor. Trying to think of ways to lessen the pain, I once bought a pair rubber gloves, the sort used for housework and washing up. We started the haul that night, me with my bright yellow hands, delighted with myself, poisoned fingers, cuts and sea boils all protected. What a relief. The only drawback was that it was going to take a while to get up to speed shaking out the fish while wearing them. 'Moogie' meanwhile (before the muck off the nets fogged his glasses right over) had his eye on me, and it wasn't long before I heard him say, "Greenwood, get those fucking gloves off," and that was it, back to the agony.

Another real bastard was the twine of the nets cutting your finger joints open. 'Sea c**ts' they were known as and, like all the other things that plagued us, there was no chance of them healing up until the weather turned poor and we had a few days in from sea. Cuts took a very long time to heal because they were opened up every night as the nets tore the scab off. When the fishing was heavy we all suffered these things, but you had to grin and bear it because the share out would be good on Saturday morning. That summer the money fell well short of the pain, however, because of the quota. It was only the sharking that made our money up.

Our bookings for sharking used to be done through Jack Bray's tackle shop, but he eventually became so exasperated with the luggers that he refused to have them on his books any more, and we all moved to Frank Hoskin's tackle shop further up the quay. This was the same chap that operated the barking boiler. The biggest problem arose when the pilchard catches were big. There, alongside the quay, shaking out their nets would be the four luggers and there was no chance they would they be finished in time to take out the anglers Frank had booked for them. He would be in his shop surrounded by 48 irate and disappointed people on a lovely summer morning, their flasks and sandwiches packed but their day out has just been cancelled. Frank must have been able to talk faster than a Philadelphia lawyer to smooth down the ruffled feathers of a mob of that size.

We came in from sea one morning ahead of a rising south-west gale. This time the catch was small and was soon put ashore, and it was 'Moogie' and Jack's turn that day to take the boat out sharking.

So just before nine o'clock our skipper jaunts into the tackle shop only to be told that because of the weather everybody has cancelled their trip. Frank was curtly informed that everybody had not cancelled their trip, and he was to round up a dozen hard asses because the *Iris* was going to sea. And go they did. The weather was atrocious, so bad in fact that 'Moogie' and Jack had to shoot a couple of nets to ride to as a sea anchor. Meanwhile ashore, the other sharking skippers were fizzing with indignation that anyone should take visitors out in near life-threatening conditions. They were going to report the *Iris* to whatever higher authority they thought might take action in such cases and when, indeed if, he got ashore they were going to tell 'Moogie' exactly what they thought of his greed for gold, etc. Just before six that evening the *Iris* arrived back in harbour safe and sound, and not a word was said or any action taken. 'Moogie' may have done wrong to take people out in such weather, but none dared tell him so to his face. Mind you, the anglers he took out that day probably holidayed for the rest of their lives in the Yorkshire Dales after that experience. Thankfully we didn't go to sea that night.

Many of the nights spent out drifting were no fun at all, but at other times it was nothing short of enchanting. Still calm nights that were totally silent, a big moon turning the sea to silver, with the fish shining in the nets, deep down in the clear dark water. Clear moonless nights, the sky studded with countless stars and the nets aglow with millions of tiny bright green jewels, flashing and sparkling as we hauled them. These 'jewels' were a form of luminous plankton that the drifter men called 'briming', and it was these tiny sea creatures that helped us to locate the shoals of pilchards.

A typical briming night would see the boat held back off the nets by a gentle breeze, the pawl on the rail roller rattling away as the head-rope and rail man haul steadily on the gear. Fish are scarce, just a few here and there along the bottom of the nets. The stower unbuttons the odd scad or mackerel from the meshes, mutters "Up, up," while the rail man shouts, "Ahead five," for a five second burst on the engine to keep the boat up to the gear. The night is very dark and our world seems to extend only as far as the working lights could penetrate into the blackness. Seagulls paddle around the boat hoping to snatch a feed, but there is precious little to be had, so even they are quiet; others on the wing enter our world from the darkness like ghosts. After four or five hours hauling, the smell of hot paraffin from the hurricane lamp on the dann marking the end of the fleet of nets wafts downwind. We will soon be 'all in'. With the last, or 'pole end' net stowed down the net room, the skipper glances around the deck. We have caught about 70 stone of fish, hardly enough to make a wage but enough to make him think there might be more about if we look around for them. There was still time, with dawn several hours away yet. So as the cook stirs up the fire to brew a pot of tea we drop the mizzen peak, the rail roller is unshipped and the shooting roller shipped up. 'Moogie' shoves the aft engine into gear and opens up the throttle, all lights including the 'nav' lights are switched off. The echo sounder in the wheelhouse, sparking away as the rotor scorches its trace onto the paper, is now the only glow of light aboard. Two men go forward to the luff of each bow to kneel on the deck, then lean on the rail to stare down into the dark water.

The old lugger bullies her way through the sea, disturbing the plankton, turning the bow wave and wake into bright green fire. Down in the water the noise of the boat scares any fish we pass over and they would panic off out of our way, activating the plankton as they go. A shark clearly outlined makes haste to clear us, mackerel dart away like miniature torpedoes, a small shoal of herrings bunches up close and dives for safety, appearing to roll as they do so. Our quarry, the pilchards, burst away in all directions looking like an under water firework display. On seeing this, the men at the bow give the skipper a shout, who confirms this sighting with the marks on the sounder paper. For a while we box around the area locating the pilchard shoals. Eventually the skipper decides it's worth shooting the nets again so around before the wind we come, the bearings of the shooting roller start to clatter as half of the fleet of nets go over the side again. Then it's hard to starboard on the wheel, and hoist up the mizzen peak, the net is dragged forward and we ride from a mooring rope made fast around it with a rolling hitch. For an hour or so we lay to the gear, the eastern sky going from black to dark grey; the night is ending and it is time to haul away again. If justice is done, another 40 or 60 stone is added to the catch, which means we have at least secured a small wage as a reward for our night's toil.

When working the drift nets, the hardest hauls we experienced were either in a dead flat calm, or a gale. In moderate weather, the motion of the boat helped us to haul the gear. As she rose on a sea, you would lay back on the net, and when she dropped away again you hauled in the slack it created. 'Let the boat do the work' was the motto. But the combination of a flat, windless sea and a spring tide guaranteed hard louster. We would be ready to shoot the nets, but in which direction? There would be nothing obvious to go by. "Put a bit more coal on the fire, Harry," says 'Moogie', hoping the resulting smoke would give a clue to a likely wind direction. No such luck, the smoke drifts skywards undisturbed. Now it was all guess work, maybe a breeze would make off from the land when the sun goes down.

A decision is made and we shoot away to the south. With the last net over the side, we come around on the swing rope and still not a breath of wind. With neither wind nor waves to make the boat pull back on the gear, the tide starts to carry the nets into big bights and whorls. This is bad news. After a quick supper the skipper decides to start the haul before things got any worse. We go to work and before you know it, the nets are leading across the bow to port. 'Tiddler' turns the head-ropes around the aft kevel (cleat) and grinds astern on the engine. After a while we come clear of the gear and start to haul away again. There is no movement in the water to help, so it's a dead haul, the rail man and the second hand on the skirt are sweating like bulls. We haul away for a net or two and things go fairly well, then they are leading down the port side again, so the roller has to be shipped up on that side and the next few nets are hauled from there. All change, and the nets are looking away from the starboard side, and it's back to working from there again. Sometimes you could have the nets right around the boat, in which case the engine was stopped for fear of wrapping the prop up. A sweep (big oar) was then shipped up on the starboard quarter, and a man had to row the lugger to her gear. It could be a long, tedious, fathom by fathom haul, and by the time the pole end buoy came over the rail we had nearly melted into our boots.

The exact opposite of that was a haul in a gale of wind. We didn't get caught out in those conditions very often because there is very little to be gained trying to work drift nets in really bad weather. The nets go up and down with the waves, making their presence known to the fish and warning them off, plus a lot of damage can be done when hauling fine cotton nets in poor weather. But anyone who goes fishing, no matter how experienced they may be, will get caught out occasionally.

It's late on a summer afternoon, and the wind is fresh south west with an angry looking sky. The shipping forecast gives better weather coming in, so this was reckoned to be the last of it. The drifters are tied along side the quay, their cabin fires lit and chimneys belching thick, yellow coal smoke. The crew men are stood around yarning, waiting to know if they are going to sea that night, but nobody is very keen; in fact most of them seemed quite intent on going home or to the pub. But the decision is taken by the skippers who were at that very moment in a huddle discussing the situation as the tide was ebbing. All of a sudden the knot of skippers splits apart, each man striding towards his boat, waving and shouting to their respective crews, by now scattered up and down the harbour: "Come on, get her ready, lets go and have a look at it," is the shout.

Many of the men aren't very happy with the decision at all. "What the fuck do they want to go out on a night like this for?" says one. "I went out the sea front, and it's looking bloody awful," says another. "Better be tied to a bull's arse and shit to death," comments another. Despite all the grumbling, the boats are quickly made ready for sea, steaming out of the harbour before the ebb tide strands them. Once out clear of the shelter of the bay there's a lot of sea running, backed up by a fresh breeze: in fact, if there was water to get back into the harbour most would have returned. But as we had scraped out on the last of the tide, there's no chance of doing that, so on we go. Perhaps the wind will decrease as the sun goes down?

Steep angry seas smack the side of the boat sending spray sweeping across the deck and all hands are dressed in oilskins, sea-boots, sou'westers and mufflers. The skipper at the wheel tries not to bury the boats head as we plunge along. All of a sudden a shout goes up: "There they are, down towards the Dodman, going down like spikes!" Somebody has seen the gannets working a shoal of fish, so we're off to investigate. Sure enough, as we approached the gannets are going crazy and there are good marks on the sounder, but are they pilchards? The gannets might have been diving on sprats or mackerel. There was one way to find out.

A gannet will swallow fish until it is too heavy to fly, then along with others in the same condition, they sit on the water paddling gently about until the meal is digested. If they have to fly, they spew up their fish to lighten themselves enough to take off, and that is when we would take advantage of them. Spying a bunch of gannets on the water, the skipper headed the boat right for them, all hands on the foredeck and as we approach the birds everyone starts screaming and shouting and waving their hats in the air. That does it; panic ensues and the birds spew up to make their escape, leaving their hard-won meal slowly sinking away. Bad news for the gannets, good news for us … it's pilchards.

'Moogie' boxes about for a while before picking his spot. Then downwind we go, the old lugger surging on the waves while the nets are flung over the side, the shooter's arms going like pistons, buoys and buffs splashing down astern of us. Riding to the gear we have a bite of supper while watching an angry looking sunset. The wind shows no sign of dropping, in fact it seems to be doing just the opposite. As soon as it gets dark the haul begins, the engine is hardly ever out of gear driving the boat up to the nets. She rises on a sea, we lay back hard on the net, then she swoops down the back of it and we haul like mad. Up she rises on the next one, and we lay back again.

The wind freshens and the seas are getting bigger. By now the aft engine throttle can't be opened up any more for fear of damaging the gearbox when working the gear leaver. So two of us nip down forward and crank up the 30 HP, the gear leaver for which comes out by the shaking boards so the stower could operate it. Away we go again, the 30 HP keeps her up to the weather, while the aft engine pushes her ahead when needed, and it's back to the routine. Up on a sea she rises. Hang on tight. There's a crash as a breaking sea bursts around us, then we slide down the back of it, bundling the net aboard while it's easy to get. The next few waves aren't so bad; the 30 HP is out of gear and we push ahead on the 45 HP, then it's ahead again on both engines as a monster sea rears up and the man out the rail yells, "Let go!" Everyone drops the net and hangs on and, despite the best efforts of both engines, the boat surfs off stern first on the wave, with the hard-won net whipping back out over the roller. The big sea roars past us, and the hauling resumes. There is no respite and, for however long it takes to gain the fleet of nets, the crew keep battling, six or seven hours non-stop, maybe longer if there is any weight of fish to be shaken out. All our strength and endurance are needed on such a night. But the drifter crews had plenty of that, and combined with pure dogged persistence the pole end buoy would eventually come over the roller.

94

The skipper then dodges the boat head to wind, the catch is scooped into boxes and lashed down, any left over is shovelled down into the fish room, the hatches shipped up and the mizzen stowed. When all is made ready, the skipper brings her around to shape a course for home. By the time the night is over and we eventually get home to bed, I feel as if I've gone ten rounds with a heavyweight boxer.

12A

Superstitions

When I first went to sea, there were old retired fishermen on the quay who remembered what life was like when they were boys at sea as far back as the 1890s. But in all their accounts of gales and hard times, none of them could recall any disasters happening to the Looe luggers. It used to be said that "God has got Looe under his wing" and I think that must have been true.

Regardless of their good record, if today's safety standards were applied to the boats of 40 years ago, none of them would be allowed to cross the harbour, let alone fight a gale, long lining 60 miles out in the Channel. One cursory inspection would have been enough to give an M.C.A surveyor apoplexy. Yet go they did, for generations, and in many cases, much further than our modern fleet goes today. But despite all today's emphasis on safety, there have been many more casualties and sinkings in the modern fleet over the past 30 years than ever there was in a century of the old fleet. So what has gone wrong? I think anybody in commercial fishing will have his own theory on that.

One thing that was rife then, and hardly exists today, was superstition. There was loads of it and it was all taken very seriously. The foremost being never to mention the word r*bb*t; for some reason they were considered to be the most unlucky of animals. Skippers have turned their boats back to harbour and tied up rather than continue at sea after that word had been mentioned.

If a net room hatch was turned upside down while being unshipped, it had to be put back the right way up immediately, spat on, and then spun around three times with the sun to undo the bad luck. After the nets were shot, the chances of a good catch could be greatly increased by throwing a coin over the side to 'buy some off Neptune'. Whistling was not allowed, for fear of whistling up the wind. Green was an unlucky colour, so no green hats, jumpers, tea mugs or even socks, nothing green at all ever. Vicars and ginger-haired or squinty-eyed women seen before going to sea were also looked upon as a bad omen. Sailors and fishermen consider the sight of a clergyman on the quay or standing near their boats very unlucky. Many will refuse to sail in the face of such an ill omen and will try to lead the minister away from the boats. Several years ago an old Polperro fisherman, Edmund Curtis, was alarmed to see a new minister to the parish had strolled innocently down to the quay to have a look round. Horrified at the thought of all the bad luck that would follow, he firmly led the minister off the quay and down Lansallos Street before he considered the danger over, politely advising the man not to return!

In some ports it is considered a bad omen to say the word 'church' or 'chapel' while at sea. I once heard about a debate on religion that once took place in the cabin of the Looe lugger *Our Daddy*. Alfred John Pengelly, the skipper, was a staunch teetotaller, a gentleman in the true sense of the word and a devout Christian. Alfred's uncle, Dorman Pengelly was one of his crew, a curmudgeonly old chap who was rather inclined to say what he thought, when he thought it and to hell with anyone who disagreed. One fine evening when the *Our Daddy* was riding to her nets and all hands were below in the cabin having a bite of supper and a mug of tea, the topic of conversation that evening touched on religion. By all accounts it got a bit heated. Dorman had not said a word until there was a momentary silence and he had a chance to air his own views on the subject.

"Anyway, when I die I want to be buried face down," was his opening line.

"Why's that then, Uncle Dorman?" said Alfred John in all innocence.

"So as the good Lord can kiss my arse," came the reply, to stunned silence from the rest of the crew. I rather think at that moment they were expecting a bolt of lightening to come through the deck striking him dead where he sat. Fortunately for Dorman, God didn't hear or chose to overlook this little outburst and he went on to live to a ripe old age, dropping dead on the quay one day while on his way to inspect a new wheelhouse being bolted down on the *Daddy*'s deck. And as far as I know he didn't get his burial request.

A superstition at Plymouth has it that if two or more things happen to go wrong while you are getting the boat ready for sea, that was it, your luck was out and you had better stay in and try again the next day. Veteran fisherman Bill Cowan related a yarn to me that took place just after he had been demobbed from the navy at the end of the last war. Bill was fishing with his uncle on the Polperro gaffer *Vilona May* working out of the Plymouth Barbican. Getting ready to go to sea one evening they had one hell of a struggle to get the engine started only to see the bow rope foul up on everything possible when it was let go. When finally they put to sea and were trying to set a bit of sail to help the old *Vilona* along, the mizzen sheet wrapped itself solidly around the outrigger. "That's it," said Bill's uncle Alfie. "We've had the warnings, our luck's out and we're going back." With that he put the tiller hard over and turned for home. Bill was wild at Alfie's decision; another nights work lost, but there was no arguing so back they went.

Back in the days when seagoing was very much a male preserve, it was considered in some ports to be a bad omen if a woman set foot aboard a boat. I rather think money cured that one however. With the growth of tourism and pleasure boating, no boatman was going to turn away a booking because the wives and girlfriends wanted to come along too. There are also many accounts of wives and daughters sailing on the ketches and schooners that traded around the coast, and I have only heard stories of how good they were, pully-hauling on deck, taking a turn at the wheel, even doing the navigation. As for cooking aboard ship, I do believe that was a male preserve. Certainly nowadays if some macho sailor or yachtie trotted out any slack-mouthed banality about women being bad luck on boats I rather imagine he would find himself going cross-eyed with agony as his knees buckled towards the deck after an indignant female foot had made firm contact with his trousers.

Going to sea in the fishing trade to earn a living is a dangerous occupation and anyone who has spent any length of time at it has had friends and acquaintances who never arrived back in harbour to land the catch that they had been so earnestly hunting. And all fishermen are well aware that every time they go fishing they are as likely as any of those that went before them to join the casualty list of men lost to Neptune. They just hope and pray that no matter how dreadful the weather they get caught out in, or how ever hair-raising and perilous the accidents that can befall a fishing vessel at sea, they will always arrive back in their home port safe, if not always sound. And thanks to long experience, good seamanship and many a silent prayer, all but a very unfortunate few do just that, trip after trip, summer and winter, year in year out.

Some boats can be unlucky, if not downright cursed, no matter who is running them or how well they are looked after. Engine trouble, electrical problems, leaks, gear loss, towed in yet again with the prop wrapped up, with them the bad luck never ends. Two such vessels spring to mind, the *Sparfell* and the *Golden Dawn*. They broke the hearts and bank balances of all the skippers who tried to earn a living with them.

Whenever and wherever folk face danger and take risks earning a living on a regular basis, superstitions abound. Last of all there is the number that comes between twelve and fourteen, as bad as those animals with the floppy ears and bobtails, so I shall say no more on the subject.

*

At the end of the 1965 pilchard season the herring nets were once more barked up and stowed aboard and, once again in the company of the *Our Boys*, we headed around Start Point for Brixham. Jack Moore had gone ashore for the winter, jowting fish around the town from our old net cart. It was the same story as the year before, shooting and hauling around Torbay and Babbacombe, mostly for very little, but persistence seemed to be the answer because we always ended up with a modest wage at the end of the week. One night we caught a few stone of pilchards, just enough to bait up the baskets of line that we carried, so 'Moogie' shaped a course up across Lyme Bay to Portland Bill where we shot the lines off Chesil Beach to catch rays. Weather wise it was a fine, clear starry sky with a light offshore wind, but it was bitterly cold. The lines were freezing in the baskets, and we were dipping up buckets of seawater to throw on the lines and to warm our hands in. Nevertheless all went according to plan and we had a good catch of fish, landing it at Brixham fish market the following day.

Brixham was like all the other fishing ports around the south west at that time, 'out on the bones of its arse'. Its fleet of trawlers was made up of a number of ex-admiralty MFVs, a few old Belgian trawlers that had come over with refugees during the war, one or two ancient motorised sailing smacks and other ageing tonnage, all rigged as sidewinders. Our interest in them extended only as far as their coal lockers, situated on deck behind the wheelhouse. In the darkness of an early morning, we would come quietly chuffing in on one engine and, going along side two or three of these trawlers, we would 'borrow' a bucket or so of coal from each of them.

One particular morning we were hitched up alongside a brand new trawler called the *Spartacus*, a pretty little craft, paintwork shining and everything in tip top order, a very rare thing in those days. On her deck were several large lumps of steam coal that had been trawled up with the catch the day before. No-one was about and the temptation proved to much for 'Moogie'. "Quick boy, nip aboard and pass them over," I was instructed. In no time at all those fine great lumps of coal were cracked up and in our locker. About an hour later the skipper of the Spartacus was aboard with a sack in his hand, muttering and cursing.

"What's up?" Moogie shouts across.

"Well," says the skipper, "I had some nice nubs of coal on deck that I was going to crack up and take up to mother, but some bastard's had them away."

"You can't trust any bugger nowadays," said Moogie. "Anyway, Harry has just made a pot of tea. Come down in to the cabin and join us for one."

"I don't mind if I do," said the skipper climbing aboard, trying to dodge the smoke swirling around our decks. It was an economical, but not a very honest way to keep the cabin stove burning (my apologies to any Brixham men reading this).

One Friday afternoon, a fresh wind was blowing right into the bay making it much to poor to go to sea. So we had fish and chips for our tea, then the five-men-and-a-bucket ablutions were performed, ready for a run ashore. Jack and I, fed up with the charms of Brixham, caught a bus to Paignton a few miles up the coast and spent the evening rambling around there for a change.

Returning to Brixham well after pub closing time, we climbed down aboard the boat and turned in, merry and well pleased with our night's adventures. 'Moogie' and Harry were already in their bunks, but there was no sign of 'Tiddler'. This was a very good thing, because if you could get to sleep before him you had a night's rest; if not, you were doomed because he snored fit to rattle the deck planks.

We were just dozing off when the man himself clambered back aboard and stumbled down into the cabin, well pissed. There was much muttering and grunting as his jacket and shoes were taken off prior to climbing into his bunk, then he decided that he needed a piddle, so up on deck he went to ease his bladder. Once relieved, there was more muttering then he started to shout and bawl that the wind had died down, the stars were shining and we really ought to be putting to sea. Harry got out of his bunk and stood in the companionway trying to coax him to come down and turn in, but he would have none of it.

"Come on, Moogie, are you afraid to go to sea or something?" he bawled loudly.

"Now, now, Tiddler, be a good boy and come and turn in," cajoles Harry.

"Turn in be buggered," says Tiddler. "There's twenty stone of herrings up in the bay for us tonight, I can feel it in my water."

"Stop being such an old twat, and let's get some sleep," shouts Jack from the depth of his bunk.

"Come on, Moogie, let's get going," came the beer soaked retort from up on deck.

This went on for about ten minutes, and all the while the skipper lay in his bunk not saying a word, but his pride would only stand so much goading no matter who was doing it, drunk or sober. Suddenly he was out of his bunk and starting up the aft engine and, to quote the old Looe shipwright, Arthur Collins, "Our hearts sank that far, you could have scooped them out of our backsides with a spoon." Away we went to sea, it must have been about one o'clock in the morning and we were all several pints the worse for wear. Of course the *Our Boys* wouldn't be left behind so out they came as well.

Steaming around the breakwater, we shipped a big sea. I was forward coiling down ropes, and got soaked. 'Tiddler' meanwhile had gone down forward to put on his oilskins, and was emerging again on deck just as the boat took it into her head to fall off a sea (she was an old cow for those sort of tricks). 'Tiddler', in his beer-soaked state, lost control and came hurtling aft, plunging onto the shaking boards, one of which promptly unshipped, and with a squawk he disappeared from view. 'Moogie' ducked out of the wheelhouse to see what had happened to him. On finding the great beer drinker down in the fish box unharmed, the skipper told him in no uncertain terms to stay where he was. Loud honking snores soon started to issue from that part of the boat.

We shot and hauled the nets twice that night and came back into harbour on Saturday morning with a miserable three stone of herrings, having suffered a cold, wet, rolling night. To add to the misery, Jack and I had been feeling very cruddy due to the stale beer sloshing around our stomachs. 'Tiddler' meanwhile was keeping a very low profile. One word from him and we would have throttled him, that is if the crew of the *Our Boys* hadn't beaten us to it.

While waiting for 'Skips' to arrive in his car, we decided to treat ourselves to breakfast of scrambled eggs up at the café. We were served up a ghastly, greenish-yellow slime on flaccid toast, ideal for the way we were feeling. While trying to eat it, I happened to mention just how bad we were going to feel on the ride home. Jack heaved and very nearly lost what he had so far managed to stuff down his neck. We were not a very cheerful bunch that morning. The ride home with 'Skips' exceeded all expectations for car sickness; twice before reaching Looe he had to pull over to let us all have a stomp around in the fresh air. Home never, ever seemed so inviting.

Returning to Brixham on Monday afternoon, we shot and hauled for another week. Thus we continued, trying to scratch a living, until the boats were steamed home for the Christmas break. Once the Christmas and New Year celebrations were over, we awaited some decent weather to allow us to return to Brixham and resume our herring drifting. It was now early January 1966 and the weather, as always at that time of year, had been boisterous to say the least. South-west gales sweeping in from the Atlantic were building up a massive swell ending in a screaming nor'westerly wind as the depression passed over, only to be followed by the next one shouldering its way in from somewhere west of Ireland. But eventually a winter anticyclone started to build and we bundled our bags down into the cabin and made the *Iris* ready for sea. A lovely winter's morning greeted us, the sky dark blue with a brassy sun shining low in the sky and, at last, a tranquil sea under a light offshore breeze. Torbay was once more our destination, but the trip was broken by a stop off at the trawling grounds south of Plymouth known as 'sleepy valley' to try for some mackerel. We had heard rumours of the Plymouth boats catching big mackerel in their trawls and so we made up a twelve-hook feather line apiece to see if we too could catch some. A couple of boxes of mackerel would be a nice boost to our herrings on Brixham market the next day.

On reaching the 'sleepy valley' grounds, the skipper proceeded to motor slowly about with the echo sounder running, looking for any signs of fish. He didn't see very much, but there were some tiny marks close to the bottom, so he stopped while we gave them a try with the lines and, much to our surprise and delight, we hauled aboard some fine big mackerel. Every time we drifted off the mark, 'Moogie' would steam slowly about until he located it again, then with the prop thrashing hard astern to stop the boat, it was away lines again, and we would soon be hauling up a fine big fish on every hook. They were so voracious, some were even dragged aboard having swallowed the lead. All day we carried on fishing in this manner and by late that afternoon 100 stone of jumbo mackerel were boxed up on deck. 'Moogie' now decided to land our catch back at Looe and try our luck out there again the next day. Torbay could wait a while. Little did we know that the herring nets were never going to be shot again.

For the next three or four days the weather held fine, and we landed a nice catch of fish each day. Come Saturday, when the money was shared out, we were very pleased with our efforts. The fish merchants had paid us £1 a stone for our mackerel, big money compared with the 3/6d we had been getting for pilchards and 6/ for herrings.

News of our success had got around, and the crews of the *Our Boys* and the *Our Daddy* also made up hand lines and joined us at sea on the next fine day. Nobody was disappointed, everyone caught prime mackerel that made top money on the market. Never had fishing been so easy or so lucrative. No shooting miles of nets or lines, nor battling for hours on end in poor weather to get the gear aboard before we could run for home. Every man simply worked a twelve-hook feather line with a 1lb lead on the end and if the weather came on too poor, it took only minuets to wind the lines back on to their wooden squares and we were ready to head for home. It was truly a revelation and, in the famous words of Harold Macmillan, 'we had never had it so good'. No one knew it then, but the beginning of one of the biggest revivals that the Cornish fishing industry had ever known, was under way. But by mid March the mackerel shoals had deserted us so it was back once more to hard labour, out in the Channel with the long lines, a world away from mackerel catching.

Our old shipmate Clarence Libby died that spring. One night he was very poorly indeed and had to leave his place on the nets. He looked dreadful, yet wouldn't go down below and lie in his bunk, insisting instead on staying in the wheelhouse, working the wheel and engine lever. When we got back into harbour he went straight home, and I never saw him again. All of us on the *Iris* attended his funeral, decked in our best sea jumpers and dark trousers, and as Clarence was originally a Polperro man he was buried in the cemetery at the top of the hill above that village. We stood with his family and friends, bare headed at the graveside, trying to blink back the tears as his coffin was lowered down. Harry gave up that struggle and just stared ahead with the tears rolling down his cheeks. A good man had passed on, and we were going to miss him a great deal.

A couple of days later we were once more out in the Channel, shooting away the lines on the 'Klondike' ground with big grey seas rolling and the gulls wheeling around us. There's a saying that when a fisherman dies he comes back as a gull, so just maybe our old shipmate was swooping by, keeping his eye on us. It's a lovely thought, returning as a gull, providing of course that you managed to keep clear of Andy on the *Endeavour* (See page 110).

14

Fog

Being caught out at sea in gales of wind, battling to retrieve the nets and lines, and fighting the weather for hours to get home to port could give us some very anxious times and were exceedingly uncomfortable to say the least, but the weather we most dreaded in those days was fog.

To the fishermen of today, fog is no big deal. Radar reveals what shipping is about and where it is. A GPS linked to a track plotter shows on screen a chart of the coast and your position to within ten feet. Take the cursor and draw a line (clear of all obstacles) from your position to your home port and steer along it, and you arrive back safe and sound. It's all good stuff, and nobody should be without it. So unless the man at the wheel makes a real hash of it, the dangers and inconveniences of fog are minimal.

The navigation methods in the 1960s were exactly the same as the 1860s, only in fog it was probably more dangerous for us because of the steamers. When putting to sea the skipper always noted the time that we cleared Looe bay, the course steered and for how long. While working the gear, if the land was visible, the compass course for home was checked regularly in case fog did close in. If the land could not be seen, the drift from wind and tide had to be estimated so that a fairly accurate course for home could be picked off. In reasonable weather conditions, any deviation could be corrected when land came in to view, or the loom of the Eddystone or Start lighthouse was sighted.

But when fog really closed in and the stem of the boat could hardly be seen from the wheelhouse, it was a very different story. The skipper would know we were so many hours steaming off the land, and the course back to harbour should be 'X', but that was the only information there was to go on. When making a passage for home in such conditions, the crew all stayed on deck, ears and eyes straining to see or hear anything that might mean danger, hands cupped to ears tracking the course of a steamer by the blast of its foghorn. A shout from the man at the stem and the skipper would wind the wheel hard down to avoid, perhaps, a trawler hauling her gear. Like a blind man crossing a busy road, we would work our way across the shipping lanes. Sometimes there was the terrifying moment when the thumping sound of a big ship's engine close at hand starts to engulf us, though often she was so near that it was hard to tell which way to go to avoid her. The tension at that moment was almost unbearable until someone shouts out, "There she is," and all eyes are suddenly riveted to the ghostly outline of a large merchant ship bashing along at a good fifteen knots only yards away as she passes, leaving us wallowing in her wake, engulfed in the thick oily smoke of her funnel. There but for the grace of God ... Stemming the wash of a vessel we had neither seen nor heard until the last moment, the danger passed, did little to soothe the nerves or the imagination. Hour after hour we stood on deck, taking turns blowing the old copper foghorn, oilskins glistening and hats sparkling with dewdrops while the cold wet fog ate into you until every bone ached.

Timing the run in, the skipper would switch the echo sounder on and when it climbed from a steady reading of 40 fathoms up to 25, we knew we were getting close to the land. The two forward engines would then be stopped, and we would proceed carefully in on the one motor until the sounder showed ten fathoms. The aft engine would be knocked out of gear and stopped. With the boat now laying still and silent on the water, everyone would cup their hands to their ears listening for any sounds that might give a clue to our position, sounds such as another vessel's engine or foghorn, waves breaking on the rocks, a dog barking on the land or, best of all, the blaring of the Looe foghorn.

If we were fortunate enough to make such a good shot of it, a couple more manoeuvres would get the foghorn bearing north-west of us, then all we had to do was steer towards the welcoming blasts to reach the harbour, safe and sound. When that happened the mood on the boat changed instantly, the tension lifted; the ordeal was over, we were now out of danger. On other occasions we might not be so lucky. Stopped on the ten fathom line in perfect silence, closely wrapped in a world of cold wet vapour with nothing to indicate direction but the compass, it almost made you dizzy. Are we east or west of Looe? That was the question. If there was a hundred yards or so visibility, the skipper might gently nudge the boat in towards the shore to get a glimpse of the rocks, their strata telling us where we were. The Oar Stone, a big rock to the west of Looe Island marks a boundary in the rock strata, looking out to sea to the west of it and back into the land to the east of it. To find Looe after that meant steering along the ten-fathom line, stopping the engine every ten minutes and listening until eventually the foghorn was heard. It was a time consuming, tedious way to gain port after a hard trip, but there were no other options. That was how it had to be done. Occasionally a boat would get totally lost and confused. The only answer then was to drop the anchor and wait for the fog to clear.

Be it gales or fog, 'Moogie' always seemed calm and collected, totally imperturbable. Later, many years into his retirement, I asked him if he was always as cool as he looked and his honest answer surprised me. "Greenwood," he said, "sometimes I was terrified!" I'm so glad I didn't know it at the time.

An accident ended our lining season early in the spring of 1966. 'Moogie' was shooting the lines away at a spanking pace when suddenly he was being dragged aft with a hook through the palm of his right hand. 'Tiddler' threw the engine hard astern and 'Moogie' managed to catch a turn of the strop around the mizzen backstay and hang on tight. The surge of the lugger still going ahead parted it. Without a second glance he ripped the hook out of his hand and carried on shooting the gear with blood going everywhere as he did so. If the turn on the backstay had been missed, our skipper would have been dragged overboard and drowned, the weight of the sinking line already shot would have ensured that. This all happened in an instant; Harry, who was standing by with the knife ready to cut away any such foul-ups, was flattened as 'Moogie' hurtled aft. His hand must have been giving him absolute hell. A three-inch conger hook, ripped out barb first, does an awful lot of damage. But 'never say die', with his right hand wrapped up in engine room rags, our skipper hauled behind the jinny for the seven hours or so that it took to get the gear in, and we finished the trip. The next day his hand was puffed up like a balloon and he had to have some time off. As it was getting near the time to start the summer drifting season, a decision was made to finish the boulter season a little early and take the old *Iris* over to West Looe for her annual paint-up.

Mike Faulkner then joined us as sixth hand. He was nicknamed 'Bushy' because of his head of curly hair. In his mid-twenties, he had started fishing when he left school, but the prospects back then had been so poor he had gone ashore to learn a trade and became a mason. With everything now looking on the up for the new winter fishery, he had decided to come back to sea again.

15

Heavy Fishing

The spring season of 1966 was one of very mixed blessings. There were plenty of pilchards up and down the coast, but we couldn't really earn any money because the canners had yet again imposed a quota on the landings. The weather was pretty blustery as well, lows coming in from the Atlantic giving us fresh south-westerly and north-westerley winds. We were making a wage each week, but everything seemed to be conspiring to prevent us making a real go of it.

During July of that summer, one of the worst sea disasters in recent times occurred off the Cornish coast. A pleasure boat from Falmouth called the *Darlwin* took guests from a hotel on a day trip to Fowey. The weather had been fine enough when they had set out but, by the late afternoon, when it was time to return to Falmouth, the wind was south-west and freshening up rapidly. Nevertheless the boat proceeded on its return voyage and was last seen bashing her way around the Dodman ... and that was it. She was never seen again, all 29 people on board were drowned and the poor, sad remains of these once happy holiday makers were brought into harbours up and down the coast as the local pleasure and fishing boats came across them. Six were brought into Looe, a very grim and haunting experience for those involved.

That dreadful disaster was the start of all the regulations for boats taking paying passengers being tightened up. Initially this meant that, for the sharking season, a life raft had to be carried. Those first rafts had copper tank floatation and were wooden slatted with a life-line around the edge, measuring about six feet by four and 18 inches deep. We could never find anywhere to stow it on the *Iris* where it wasn't in the way. Later, proper inflatable life rafts packed in an oilskin valise became available, but they were still big, heavy, awkward things to find stowage for. After dragging their life raft around the deck and finding nowhere suitable to lash it down, the crew of the *Our Boys* eventually solved the problem by squeezing it down through the cabin hatch and stowing it in a bunk. Ideal!

That season we worked a fleet of 22 nets, and some of them were very long nets indeed. The average drift net was 90 fathoms long, kept afloat by twelve buoys and three buffs, but some of the nets 'Moogie' put together required 18 buoys to keep them afloat. The hurricane lamp lashed on the pole end dann looked to be nearly out of sight when we came around on the swing rope. The other drifters worked fleets of between twelve and 15 nets of a standard length. Many is the night I have watched them get underway for home when we still had half our fleet to haul. By the time our last net came over the roller most of the other boats had landed their fish and their crews were home, snug in bed. One big annoyance of being the last boat out was ending up with all the gulls. The air around every drifter used to be full of them, screaming and fighting for fish. But when a boat put its working lights out to steam for home, they soon realised there was nothing more to be had and would flock to anyone still working. So the last poor buggers hauling (and it was usually us) had to work in a blizzard of screaming, shitting birds.

Andy Andrews, the head rope man on the *Endeavour* devised a method of keeping them at bay. It was effective, but it remained unique to Andy. He would snatch a gull out of the air and throw it down on the deck beside him. The *Endeavour*'s bulwarks were high and the working area for the head rope man was narrow, so there was no way that a gull could make its escape. But seagulls are very bold creatures and, after recovering from the initial shock of capture, a few ruffled feathers would be preened back into place and it was soon gorging on fresh pilchards. That was until it was time for this unfortunate bird to star in its new role. When the other gulls started to make too much of a nuisance of themselves, Andy would snatch this poor creature up off the deck and, brandishing it aloft in his left hand, the gnarled index finger of his right was inserted firmly up its little feathered jacksy. The squawk of pain and terror it let out was enough to keep the rest away for quite a while. By the time the *Endeavour*'s crew hauled their last net over the rail, Andy's victim of the night must have had the sorest bum of any bird in the world, proving conclusively that there really is no such thing as a free lunch.

Anyone who crewed on the *Iris* really knew the meaning of hard work. She had a long established record for being a workhorse. 'Moogie' Frank, as with his father 'Moogie' Tom who was skipper before him, always pushed the limits of what could be achieved. If a younger, stronger man joined the crew such as Mike Faulkner, filling the gap once held by an older, slower man, then the nets or lines would be lengthened out to keep everyone at their limit. If you could stick it, there was a big difference in the money shared at the end of the week compared with some of the other boats. Mind you, big catches didn't always mean big money.

Pilchard fishing up and down the coast had been heavy, so the cannery once again put us on a 120 stone per boat quota until they had cleared the backlog a bit. One evening aboard the *Iris*, riding to the nets deep off Fowey, we were looking forward to a quick mug of tea and going to work before too many fish poked their heads in the meshes. Jack and I had taken people out sharking during the day and now, on our second night without any sleep, we were hoping for an easy haul and an early night in. 'Moogie' had gone forward to make the swing rope fast on the kevel when he noticed the buoys nearest the boat had started to bob, indicating that a shoal of fish had hit in hard. There was no time for our supper, we donned oilskins and started the haul there and then while the sun was still up in the sky over the western land.

This first shoal went from the top to the bottom of the boat net. The head ropes and skirt were put together, the whole thing being about as big around as a dustbin, and all hands on the foredeck hauled until our eyes bulged to inch it over the rail. Spreading the net, foot by foot, the pilchards were shaken out, then we strained to haul a couple more fathoms aboard and do the same again. There was to be no let up, the shoals were hitting in hard all along the nets.

The tea that Harry had brewed when the nets were first shot was eventually drunk some time in the early hours of the following morning where we stood, up to our knees in pilchards, attached to the deck as firmly as if we were standing in wet concrete. Eleven nets were cleared and stowed, the remaining eleven were 'boarded in', which meant hauling as fast as possible and shaking out what fish you could without breaking the rhythm. The nets, fish and all, were then piled into the net-room to be run out and cleared once back in the harbour. It took ten hours non-stop to get the pole end buoy over the roller (the sun was now well up over the eastern land), the nets and fish were piled up like a haystack and we had to wrestle them about so that the skipper could see over the top to steer. Then, with the governors on the engines lashed back to make all speed, we just managed to save our tide back into Looe. The *Iris* was the only boat that night to have heavy fishing. The *Endeavour* had even shot a second time to try and make her quota up, steaming along a berth off our port side with us shouting that we had plenty and not to bother. However, her old Bolinder engine made so much noise it was like being in the company of a Shackleton bomber, so it was hardly surprising that her crew didn't hear us.

With the ropes ashore in the harbour, we boxed up and landed our 120 stone of fish. It was then time for a much-needed breakfast in one of the quayside cafes. Revived by a good fry up and a couple of mugs of tea, it was then back to work. We had caught a huge catch of fish but unfortunately we had no market for it. To clear the decks a bit Henry Dunn, one of the local farmers, arrived and took a trailer-load away at a knock-down price to use for fertilizer. Then, with the roller and spars rigged athwartships, we proceeded to 'shake out'. It was mid-afternoon before the last fish were shaken out and the nets salted and stowed back down the net-room. To get rid of the deck-full of unwanted pilchards, the boat was steamed out into the bay and there, with the wheel lashed hard to starboard, they were scooped over the side as she motored in circles. By this time even the gulls weren't interested; most of them couldn't even fly, let alone swallow any more fish.

We scrubbed the old *Iris* from end to end and, just before the hatches were shipped up, 'Moogie' rather lamely suggested that we go out and shoot away again so as not to miss that night's quota and wash the nets out. I rather think he knew what our reply would be, because within ten minutes we were in harbour tied up.

On that trip we had hauled by hand two miles of net, nine fathoms deep, containing an estimated twelve tons of fish. Every single fish had been flipped, twisted and shaken out of the meshes, and we had worked non-stop for over 20 hours to do it. The cannery had taken three quarters of a ton, the farmer had taken about two tons, we had dumped over nine tons out in the bay and for all our labours we had earned about £4 each.

We were all toughened up to hard physical work and had become used to going without any real sleep for long periods of time. But there was definitely a limit to how long anyone could keep going for. It varied from person to person, but once that line was crossed, wherever it may lie, you were venturing into very uncertain territory. We could all work for 36 or 40 hours at a stretch without any apparent ill effects. You looked haggard and felt worn right out, but a good kip and a decent meal would soon put you back to rights. It was on the occasions that even those hours were exceeded that strange things could start happening. Hallucinating was one effect.

Steaming out one evening, 'Tiddler' rushed down forward and jammed the engines hard astern, stopping the boat dead, before emerging back upon deck in a real sweat, shouting, "Don't any of you bastards keep your eyes open? Did none of you see that?" The sea was glassy calm, the sun was shining and there was nothing around us for miles. Nobody said anything more than, "I think its gone now, Tid," and he went below and put the engines back into gear and opened up the throttles again. I clearly remember driving home one morning and slamming on the brakes to avoid a rocking chair that leaped out of the hedge in front of me. It was all very weird.

The zombie effect was another result of staying awake too long. When that happened, your brain just went on strike; someone had to pass you your mug of tea and then make sure that you drank it, otherwise you just sat there staring out with it in your hands. When it was time to haul, whoever was suffering had to be helped on with their oilskins and put to their place on the nets. Working at a steady pace he would be fine, but if a splat of fish come aboard and the rhythm was broken while it was being shaken out, he would be unaware of it and try to carry on in the same way until he was brought too by a shout. Some men were tougher than others, but I think most of us experienced that sort of thing once in a while when the going got really hard.

My poor mother used to get quite upset at the state I used to arrive home in, and many is the time that I didn't get home at all. If the fishing was heavy it was just too much effort to get back home to Talland for a few hours rest before going back to Looe again in the evening. It was much easier just to collapse into my bunk aboard the boat. If we had managed to land the catch in time, a couple of the crew may well have taken the boat out again with a load of anglers. If that was the case, I would go up to the net loft and crash out on the nets; after so many hours on my feet it was utter bliss just to lie down, close my eyes and sleep regardless of the surroundings.

The combination of fine summer weather and good fishing meant we had to go for it while the going was good. After one such spell, when we had seen every sunrise and sunset for a fortnight and I hadn't been home for nearly a week, we were alongside the quay shaking the nets out when Mum arrived at the quayside having caught the bus in to Looe to search for her long lost son. She was not happy: "Where the hell have you been for the last week? I have cooked dinners for you that have all gone to waste, you haven't phoned to say what has been happening. I didn't know if you were alive or dead". That sort of performance from your mother in front of everyone makes you feel about two inches tall. But she did have a very good point, so I apologised to her and explained about the heavy fishing and that I wouldn't be home that day either, as another catch had yet to be landed and we were away again on the next tide. It was after that incident that Mum gave up; she expected me when she saw me, and hoped for the best when she didn't.

When I did arrive home, the whole family knew about it because the stench of pilchards and diesel was strong enough to very near clear the house. In addition, fish scales drying and falling off my clothes left a trail wherever I went. Because of this odour and litter problem, I was given a bedroom with its own door onto the courtyard and forbidden from entering the house in my work clothes.

The summer of 1966 was the first time that radio communication was tried out by the Looe fleet, only to be silenced later by due process of the law. It all started with a chap called Bill Breeze. Bill owned an engineering works at Bakewell in Derbyshire, but lived in semi-retirement in Looe. A sociable type, he would stroll around the quay chatting to one and all, and he loved to go out on the boats. Day trips, angling, out by night on the drifters and, to avoid his mother-in-law, he even went long lining. In return, if any skipper had trouble getting parts for an engine, he would have them made at his factory at no charge - a very useful man to know.

One Saturday he came jaunting down the quay with a couple of hand-held walkie-talkies of Japanese manufacture. He demonstrated them over the length of the harbour and everybody was duly impressed. They had a range of five miles or so, and their usefulness on a boat didn't need spelling out. As Bill offered to supply them at a very reasonable price, all the lugger skippers and most of the shark boat skippers ordered one there and then. A couple of weeks later the new toys arrived and, as radio communication was something few had experienced, the airwaves were red hot before the novelty wore off. Alfred John of the *Our Daddy*, who had a lovely singing voice, serenaded us one evening with 'Lower Lights' and 'Will Your Anchor Hold', two of the fishermen's favourite hymns, while other singers in the fleet warbled some old music hall favourites with much banter and chit chat in between. All in all, those little radios were a great hit.

But the bubble was soon to burst. The Post Office, then in charge of radio communication, started picking up all this chatter and sent letters to all concerned, warning them that they were broadcasting without a licence, and even if a licence was applied for it could not be granted as the sets were broadcasting on an illegal waveband. 'So be good boys and pack it up right now, or else' was the gist of the warning. Several such warnings were issued, but all to no avail, the radios remained as popular as ever. However it all came to a head late one afternoon as the angling boats were coming in from sea. Each one was boarded and the offending radios were confiscated in a James Bond-style raid. Later a summons was issued to all the skippers to attend the magistrates' court at Liskeard. On the appointed day and hour, the radio pirates of Looe stood before the man on the bench who gave them the waggly finger, and fined them ten pounds each.

Silence reigned once more over the airwaves, and it was to be another seven or eight years before the small, and legal, marine VHF radios started to be come available.

That summer I had the job on the nets as stower, not generally a popular berth. You had to be very quick handed, unmeshing mackerel and scads, clearing conger drills and anything else that the other crew members had passed on rather than break the pace of the haul. These drills were caused by the conger swimming up from the bottom to help themselves to supper. Their calling card would be about four inches of net wound up tight and covered in slime. The stower was also responsible for the boat's trim, which meant stowing the net evenly across the width of the net room to prevent an unwanted list. Working such a big summer fleet, one net stowed incorrectly meant the hatches wouldn't ship up. 'Bushy' didn't want the job so he took my place out the rail and I went as stower. I stayed in that berth until I left the *Iris* three seasons later. It was a job I quite liked. Whereas the rail berth was all muscle and louster, stowing required a fair bit of skill, swishing the net evenly out the port and starboard wings of the net room as flat as a billiard table. Shirking up the rest of the crew with "Up, up," when your bit of net was cleared, getting the timing right and there was a bit of fun to be had at the expense of our poor cook. When a fish was flipped down the net room I would shout, "Net room," and Harry would have to jump down and get it. Before leaping, he momentarily balanced on the coamings, steadying himself with the engine gear lever. If the timing was right, then a split second after he let go of the lever to jump 'Bushy' would shout, "Go ahead". Harry would attempt to turn in mid air to snatch at the lever, but always missed it, and would land in a heap down on the nets. If I thought I could get away with it then I would 'accidentally' throw a fang of net right over him, pretending not to have seen this. There he would be, cursing and swearing, having lost his hat and fag all soggy, trying to get the fish and crawl out from under the net all at the same time. On deck we would be silently splitting our sides at his antics. 'Moogie', staying deadpan, would add to it by bellowing, "For fuck's sake, Harry, what are you pissing around at? Chuck that bloody fish up and get out the way". The poor old bugger, we had to treat him nicely for a while after that.

The downside of being the stower was when there was a heavy plankton bloom in the sea, 'cow shit water' it was known as. Plankton washing through the nets on the tide would stick to them in their billions, making the twine look about three times as thick. When hauled, the nets were a mass of green-brown slime and with all the flapping and shaking, the air would be full of it. The stower, who stood down on the fish box shaking boards about a foot lower and a bit aft of the rest of the foredeck crew – and, of course, working up head to wind - was in pole position for anything airborne. By the time the last net came aboard on a night when the 'cow shit water' was about, my oilskins and hat would be running with this slime, and my face set rigid behind a claylike mask where my body heat had dried it on. Everyone had their share of this stuff, but the stower had double. Mind you, when it came to green slimy hats, everybody on the drifters had one, 'cow shit water' or not. Because we all wore long oilskin jumpers it was nearly impossible to get to your hankie so if you needed to wipe your face or blow your nose, the easiest thing to hand was the inside of your hat (because the outside was always wet).

During the summer months, swarms of jellyfish would drift up Channel on the warm Gulf Stream and there were many different types. Brown umbrella-striped ones the size of a large mushroom, transparent purple-tinted ones the size of a tea plate, and white opaque ones, the bodies of which could be as big as a dustbin lid. They all pulsated along in an aimless sort of way, each one towing behind it several feet of sting-laden, jelly-like tentacles with which they caught their prey. Of course when they came up against our nets, an awful lot of the tentacles got caught in the meshes and the jellyfish would swim on leaving them behind. By the time a few thousand of these creatures had all suffered the same accident, the nets would be liberally coated from end to end in what we called stingers, and sting they did. In clearing the nets of fish, every shake and flap sent these still active tentacles flying about. A single sting was not very startling, it felt like a very mild nettle. But repeated hundreds of times over several hours and your face, hands and forearms began to feel as if they were on fire.

16

A New Fishery

By mid October the pilchard season was drawing to a close, so the nets were hauled ashore, dried out, and stowed up in the store for the winter. The herring nets were left where they were, as we didn't intend to go to Brixham. Mackerel fishing was the new winter occupation, and all around the harbour boats were making ready. Shoals of mackerel were coming on to the coast from Plymouth to Newlyn. Where they came from and why, nobody knew, but come they did. After years of stagnation and decline the fishing harbours along the south Cornish coast were coming back to life. From barely scratching a living in the winter, we were now earning good money. 'Moogie' even got so keen that we went to sea on Boxing Day.

This was a brand new fishery and there was much to be learnt about it. We started off using 1lb lead weights and a dozen feathers on a hand line. Hauling the line up in a fresh wind, it would get blown around the deck and tangle up, bights of it would wrap around your boots or mackerel flapped around in it. Either way it was the devil of a job to keep clear. Hauling it into a fish box helped, but it wasn't really the answer. A line full of big mackerel could swim around with your lead weight, sometimes leading to every one of the crew tangled up together in a real 'bunch of bastards'. The hydraulic gurdy and line stripper were still way off in the future. There were also big shoals of pollack about at that time, and if we dropped our lines into them everything was parted away in an instant. Do that three or four times and it was time to go home as there would be nothing left to tie on the lines. Sharks were another menace. But despite all the frustrations, those first couple of winters laid the foundations for one of the biggest revivals the Cornish fishing industry had ever seen.

The gurdy (a wheel of 18 inches or so in diameter clamped to the rail and turned by a handle) was one of many improvements introduced: the line was wound on to it, doing away with all the tangles. The sets of feathers became 24 hooks long made of heavy-duty gut, and the leads to sink them with now weighed 3lbs each. Catches started to exceeded 100 stone per man instead of per boat, as when we first started.

With so many boats fitting out in Looe for the winter mackerel fishery, the old fish market truck driven by the market manager, 'Shakes', could no longer handle it all. It was going up to Plymouth market perilously loaded, sometimes doing two or three runs. To ease the situation, Ray Pettier, the local coal merchant, stepped in with his lorry. After a day on the coal round, he would hose it down to get the coal dust off before loading up with boxes of mackerel to take to the market in the morning.

Young men were starting to trickle back into the industry and boats that hadn't had a fish on their decks in 20 years were being refitted and sent back to sea. Hippies, Spanish waiters and even farmers were getting in on the act - one lot used fertiliser bags cut up as oilskins and even had their dog with them. Initially they caught few fish, but they did provide a lot of entertainment and suffered much ribald commentary. To be fair, some of these more unlikely characters did stick it out, and several of them became damn good fishermen. Mackerel fishing on the *Iris* was like any other form of fishing on the boat, it was done to the maximum. If the fish were biting, then we worked non-stop right through the day; the gallon water-can would be passed around but that was it as far as refreshment was concerned. We used to feel quite envious watching the other crews belaying up for ten minutes or so, enjoying a mug of tea and a sandwich. But we were usually the top boat and in our skipper's eyes, that was what it was all about.

The Christmas holiday lasted all of two days that year and we were back to sea again on Boxing Day. New Year's Day 1967 was celebrated with a deck-full of mackerel. If the weather was workable and the fish were biting, there was no let up. 'Moogie' was the ultimate fisherman, and I think that if anyone had tried to work in worse weather or longer hours than he did they would have either sunk their boat, or dropped dead from exhaustion. We carried on in this manner until the mackerel shoals left the coast in early March. Then, in a more or less seamless change over, ten driftnets were stowed down into the net-room as a bait fleet, and the decks were jam-packed with baskets of line. It was time once again to do battle out in the Channel, after conger, ray, ling and pollack.

Nowadays the fish room of a modern fishing vessel is well insulated and the catch is gutted, washed and iced to ensure it stays in prime condition for the market. That, however, was not the way of things on the luggers. The fish room or fish box, as it was called, was beneath the shaking boards where the unhooker worked. It was divided into three pounds, one for conger, one for rays and one for white fish such as ling, pollack and whiting. There was no insulation of any sort on the *Iris*; the top section or the forward bulkhead was open to the engine room, so for the six or eight hours of the return trip with the hatches shipped up, the engines chuffed away keeping the temperature up nicely. But ray and conger take a long time to die, in fact, some would still be showing signs of life when being landed, so maybe that was how we got away with it. Nevertheless that sort of treatment can't have done much for the quality of the fish, but nobody seemed to worry; it had always been done that way.

As the line was hauled, the gaffer hooked the big fish aboard, telling the man behind the jinny to ease up as he did so. With smaller fish, he just caught hold of the strop and passed them over the hauler heads. The unhooker then dangled the fish over the appropriate pound and with his T-hook (an unhooking tool), flipped it off the hook and down it went. Mind you, a 70 or 80 pound conger could take a bit of dealing with. Sometimes they weren't even hooked but were caught because they had swallowed a smaller hooked conger. Once gaffed aboard, they would spit out the smaller conger and then go ramping around the deck in a really evil temper. After a bit of a fight we would get them below where they would slither about barking and swallowing whip congers that would wriggle around in their guts and then pop back out through their gills. Occasionally, one of these big eels would lever its tail under the parting boards and unship them, with the result that all the fish would then be mixed up and someone had to go down there and sort them out again. This had to be done with care, because if a big conger got a grip you were in trouble. They could drill a finger off at the knuckle very easily, and there was nothing you could do that would make them let go. Severing the head from the body with a sharp knife was the only answer.

On one trip a couple of bottom boards unshipped and all the congers escaped down into the bilge. What a state they were in by the time we had gaffed them out from amongst the ballast and under the engines. They took a fair bit of scrubbing up before they could be landed.

Back in harbour, the catch would be tossed up on deck where it was gutted and washed, then flung up on to the quay to be graded, boxed and weighed ready for the market. After landing, the fish box had to be scrubbed out, a filthy job because bucketsful of slime mixed up with shit and old bait had to be scooped and passed up before the scrubbing out could commence, and the stench was eye watering.

That season I was given the dubious honour of looking after the line hauler or jinny as it was called. Like the rest of the boat, it was pretty much clapped out. Lurking in a box beneath the hauler head was its 'Brit' three HP petrol engine; a magneto provided a spark for the plug, and a brass oil chest provided lubrication to the bearings through wicks and pipes. It had been bolted to the deck on the luff of the starboard bow sometime in the early 1920s and in its time it had been a good old servant, but had now grown rather cantankerous with age. It was what was known as a one-man engine, because all its little foibles had to be known and catered for if it was to start and, hopefully, stay running. When it was primed and ready, a handle was engaged to the very worn dogs in the centre of the flywheel. There was not a lot of compression to worry about, so you cranked away, going faster and faster. It would begin to fart and splutter, but still you had to keep winding until, if it fancied the idea, it would eventually pick up and chuff away, emitting clouds of sickly exhaust fumes laden with unburned petrol. Sometimes it took three or four goes to get it running and as many changes of spark plug, each one heated up and pencilled.

Stopping dead while hauling the line was one of the jinny's more exasperating habits. Two men would then have go to the rail and haul by hand (the strain of it nearly glazing their eyes over) until it could be coaxed back into life again. Backfiring on one occasion, it bounced the starting handle overboard off my forehead, giving me a tidy gash. Luckily I was only giving it a test run in the harbour and I managed to retrieve the handle at low tide. I suppose a new set of piston rings and reseating the valves would have cured most of the problems, but that didn't seem to be the way of things in those days.

We said goodbye to the *Guide Me* that summer. Ned, her skipper, had passed on and after the funeral his widow put the old lugger up for sale. A local publican bought her, and the crew continued to run her, skippered by 'Waller' Pengelly. But it didn't work out. Her engines were worn out, her nets were in rags and she was leaking badly. Without massive reinvestment (and that was out of the question) she could not continue, so she was put up for sale again. Amazingly she soon found new owners, and one fine afternoon in late August we watched her steaming out of the harbour, the decks cluttered with all her gear. She was on passage to St Peter Port in the Channel Islands where she was refitted to work as a crabber.

And so the seasons rolled on, long-lining in the spring, pilchard drifting in the summer and back to mackerel fishing in winter. 'Moogie's son Mike left school and joined the crew, keeping up a family tradition that had gone on for generations. Poor Mike suffered with seasickness as bad, if not worse, than I had but his father showed him no mercy. It was the same old treatment: "Come on, my sonny, up off your knees and catch hold the nets, work it off." "A quick hand for a scabby arse," "Rattle your dusters," and "John Edward is looking at you," etc. When I think about it now, a 15-year-old kid being goaded along through seasickness, trying to work and stay awake sometimes for 20 or 30 hours on the trot is almost unbelievable by today's standards, but back then there were men at sea who had gone through the same thing when they were only twelve years of age, a tough start to a hard life.

Steaming out to shoot the nets one summer's evening, we were on deck making ready when something, I can't remember what, went wrong. There was an awful lot of effing and blinding going on and our skipper obviously thought that this was not suitable language for his young son to hear. With a face like thunder, he poked his head out of the wheelhouse window and, glaring at us over the top of his glasses, bellowed, "And you lot can stop that fucking swearing!" Nobody laughed, we didn't dare, but he knew and we knew that our captain's attempt to capture the moral high ground had nose-dived to earth. The swearing continued unfettered and the subject was never raised again.

In the spring of 1968, with the good prospect of the winter fishery, and his son's future to think about, 'Moogie' ordered a new boat from Curtis & Pape, a boatyard situated up the West Looe river. Designed by Alan Pape, the yard boss, she was to be 38 feet long, with a forward wheelhouse and a hatch board deck working area. Packing two powerful modern diesel engines and a top of the range echo sounder, plus radio and autopilot, she proved to be a fine craft. I was supposed to be joining her as one of the crew, but that was not to be.

I had always fancied the idea of doing some time under sail in a big sailing vessel of some kind. So when the opportunity arose, I jumped at the chance of a trip on the newly launched STA vessel *Sir Winston Churchill*. She was a three-mast topsail schooner, 150 feet long and 300 tons. Operated as a youth training ship she took young people between 16 and 21 years of age on two-week character building cruises. Sailing as a trainee on her maiden voyage in March 1966, I thoroughly enjoyed myself and was asked back again to sail as watch leader for another two weeks in 1967. In early 1968 I sailed once more as watch leader, this time for a five-week stint. But that was going to be it; financing the trips and taking time off from the fishing was costing me too much money.

Then, out of the blue, I received an offer to sail as full-time bosun on the *Churchill*'s newly-launched sister ship, the *Malcolm Miller*. This was much too good an opportunity to pass up, so in October 1968 I left the *Iris* and joined the STS *Malcolm Miller* at Millbay Docks, Plymouth. My drifting days were now over. Most people sailing aboard these schooners considered themselves to be leading a fairly tough life. There were no winches, everything was haul and drag, there was plenty of sea time, and both vessels were as wet as hell in bad weather. But after four and a half years on the *Iris*, life on the *Malcolm Miller* seemed like one long holiday to me.

The first skipper I sailed under was Glynn Griffiths, a quietly spoken Welshman who ran his ship in a happy easy-going manner. He never overlooked the fact that sailing was the first and foremost object of the exercise: but birthdays were remembered and celebrated, there would be drinks all round for the permanent crew after battling a gale of wind and fancy dress parties and musical evenings were held on fine nights at sea. The rigours of sail training were leavened with good humour.

I well remember my 21st birthday, the 30th of October 1968. We were crossing the Irish Sea from Dublin, making to round Lands End and then up the Channel to Portsmouth. It was the sort of day that, on a sailing ship, you just let pass and hope tomorrow will be better; the wind was blowing south-west force six to eight, with decks awash and plenty of spray and rain. As for it being my birthday, I thought maybe I would take a run ashore and celebrate it in our next port of call. But the day suddenly took a turn for the better. To my surprise, I was called up to the chartroom where, to the popping of champagne corks, the captain and officers wished me a happy birthday and presented me with an engraved tankard and a card signed by all of the crew. Braced against the Atlantic rollers that were flooding the deck as they passed us by, we drank champagne, ate nibbles and made small talk. It was a very memorable party, and I treasure that tankard still.

Captain George Shaw was the second skipper I sailed under. He ran his ship in a very different way. A dour Scot and as hard as nails, who believed that life was not to be enjoyed, it was to be endured. He was a first class sailor, of that there was no doubt, and providing the kids understood that they had come for two weeks sail training and not for two weeks fun, then they were okay. The maximum sail was always carried in the conditions then prevailing. He never sought shelter in bad weather, and we always left port on the appointed hour, no matter what the conditions were at sea. Double reefed mizzen and staysail was the rig of the day for force nine and above. In those extreme conditions we worked the ship with water up to our waist and breaking over our heads. Big seas would smash aboard, forcing gallons of water through the vents and hatches turning the companionway ladders into waterfalls. The galley fire would be out, and we lived in our wet clothes and oilskins. While the gale lasted all would be dank and miserable. But to be honest, those conditions were usually only met with at either end of the sailing season, March and April or October to December. Most of the time we sailed about perfectly safe and dry. But Captain Shaw seemed to like nothing better than to pit himself and his ship against a bit of bad weather if there was any to be had.

We voyaged from the Baltic to the Bay of Biscay and all around the British Isles as far north as the Shetlands. It was a fantastic experience but it was quite trying after a while. Thirty-nine young people arrived aboard every fortnight, and for the first few days they would be a danger to both themselves and the ship. Then, just as they were starting to learn the ropes and become a bit useful, their fortnight would end and after a hectic weekend turn around, we would begin all over again. And apart from six weeks home leave a year, I had no life other than the ship.

I finally signed off the *Malcolm Miller* in 1973 and came home again to Looe and the fishing. By then things had changed out of all recognition. It was fast becoming a young man's world, fishing families were buying their own homes, driving cars and going on holiday. New boats were under construction at the local yards, while many of the older ones had been refitted and re-engined. The winter mackerel fishery had by now expanded into a huge county-wide industry employing over 300 boats, anything from 18 foot cove boats, to 60 foot Newlyn long-liners. After years of near stagnation, coves and quays, ports and harbours throughout the county had come back to life. Ashore, teams of people were employed each evening packing the fish into boxes, weighing and then loading them into the refrigerated lorries that took this fresh Cornish produce all over Europe.

Either side of the mackerel fishery, methods of fishing new to Cornwall were being tried out such as scallop dredging, tangle netting and trawling. It was all upbeat and go-ahead, so very different from ten years before. In Looe, 'Moogie' in his new boat *Ganesha* was top skipper, still working hours that few could stick in weather that most men were happy to ride out under the lee of a pub bar. There were one or two skippers like him in every port. They were the leaders (some called them greedy bastards), and they dragged the others along in their wake. Many is the poor weather day that the fleet landed a good catch, but initially no one would have ventured out if the top men hadn't cast off and lead the way.

17

A New Role

By the mid 1970s the old men and their luggers had all but faded from the scene, retiring with honour and dignity. They had kept the spark of a once great industry alive through many bleak years; now it was the turn of the young men joining this new, up-and-coming industry to restore the fortunes of the Cornish fishing ports, and they have done so magnificently.

Around the Cornish coast a handful of the better luggers did carry on working, but not in their old trade. They were refitted to go trawling, mackerel fishing, crabbing and wreck netting. Some remained working into the 1980s, two or three even survived into the 1990s. By then, in amongst the modern fishing boats now mainly constructed from either glass fibre or steel, they looked like something that had escaped from a maritime museum. But everyone loved to see those gallant old survivors still earning a living from the sea. One of the very last luggers fishing commercially was the *Happy Return*, built at Porthleven in 1906 and later renamed *Britannia*. She worked out of Weymouth as a crabber, landing her final catch in the spring of 1998.

That could well have been the end of the story. Four hundred years of service now encapsulated in the past, preserved only in museum models, pictures and old photographs. Happily that was not the way things turned out. If the last luggers had been withdrawn from service in the 1950s, I doubt any would be around today. But as with vintage cars or antique furniture, the secret of survival is to get past the stage of being considered as nothing more than old fashioned, worn out and fit only for scrapping. But the stark fact was, after so many years of hard usage and frugal maintenance, these boats were not in any way fit for further service.

126

A lugger at the end of her working days would usually be making a fair amount of water through the hull. Her deck would also be leaking and probably sagging in reverse camber, with depressions worn in it over the years by the boots of the crew standing at their work stations. Bulwarks so shaky that a boy could have knocked them asunder with a 2lbs pound hammer. Gribble worm in the keel, and most of the iron bolts and fastenings in the hull rusted to danger point and beyond, and that was only for starters. A detailed survey would usually show that she was so far gone as to be well beyond economic repair.

But a new generation of leisure sailors had come into being who weren't interested in the latest super-efficient, sleek, factory built sailing machines in shining-white fibreglass. No, these 'classic boat' enthusiasts had an eye to history and wanted vessels from the age of working sail. The words 'beyond economic repair' held no terrors for such people. They spent, and still do spend, thousands of pounds and hours to match, rebuilding a boat from the keel up, if that's what it takes to get an historic craft back to sea once more. They come from all walks of life, from every trade and profession, and it is thanks to them that so many of Britain and Europe's traditional sailing vessels have been brought back to life.

So, for the surviving luggers, salvation was at hand; their good looks, fine lines and legendary sailing qualities had not escaped the notice of these people. Because they are now scattered world wide, it is very difficult to say exactly how many Cornish luggers are still in existence today, but I estimate it to be 60-plus and, of them, probably 30 or more are in sea-going order. The oldest is the *Barnabas* of St Ives, built in 1881; the youngest of the originals is the motor lugger *Lindy Lou*, built at Looe in 1947. But the tally is always on the increase, as news from somewhere in the British Isles, Europe or even America comes in of some long-forgotten craft, putting yet another name back on to the list. Typically, she is either somebody's well maintained pride and joy or a sorry old bundle of sticks that some brave soul has every prospect of breaking both their heart and bank balance in rebuilding. But without these people there would be very few traditional boats on the water.

An example of this is the crabber from Weymouth, the old *Britannia*. After 92 years service she was shattered and, to save her from the chainsaw, a group of friends in Penzance formed the Mount's Bay Lugger Association to raise the many thousands of pounds necessary to finance her rebuild. Now back under her original name and dipping lug rig, the *Happy Return* sails the seas once more and is (we hope) good for another hundred years. Another is the *Ripple*, a St Ives lugger built in 1896 and owned by John Lambourne of Newlyn. Having established a temporary yard on Newlyn quay, he and his shipwrights are now undertaking her restoration. Two new luggers have been launched in recent years: in 1993 Norman Laity and friends built the *Dolly Pentreath* of St Ives, 34 feet long with dipping lug rig. Skippered by Norman's son Mike, she takes summer visitors on trips around the bay and occasionally takes part in sailing regattas. In August 2004, Jane Hayman and Marcus Rowden launched the 32 foot *Veracity* at Dartmouth that they had built her themselves with help and advice from local shipwright Brian Pomeroy. An exact replica of the original lugger of the same name, she carries a dipping lug rig and has no engine, therefore joining the elite company of the *Guide Me, Reliance, Pet* and the *Vilona May*, the pure sailers of the fleet.

Technically a sailing vessel is known by its rig, and among the luggers there are a number sporting a gaff rig as well as those with dipping and standing lug rigs. But it is what they were, and the family of boats that they belong to, that ensures they are still classed as luggers. Every summer they can be seen racing at the classic boat regattas around the coast of the Westcountry and over in Brittany, and they remain some of the fastest pieces of wood on the water. Many a smartly-attired yachtsman has been amazed (not to say well choked-off) by having his expensive piece of polished plastic overhauled by an ancient lugger, crewed by a hairy-arsed bunch in tatty smocks. These vessels are not just confined to jaunting around the coast on fine summer days. Some very serious voyages have been undertaken in a few of them, and doubtlessly there will be more in the future.

The *Vilona May*, 28 ft and built in Looe in 1896 is strongly rumoured to have made a voyage to Australia in the mid 1950s, although I haven't seen any solid evidence of it. She has cruised around Europe extensively; rig, gaff cutter and no engine. Latterly rebuilt and skippered by Chris Rees of Millbrook, Cornwall. In November 2005 he and his family sailed the Atlantic to winter in the West Indies before voyaging up to Boston. Chris was then joined by

Graham Butler and together they headed up to Greenland before Chris undertook the three week voyage back to Cornwall single-handed; the only mishap occurred in fog at night when the bowsprit struck an iceberg.

The *Lily*, 28ft and built in Looe in 1898 was renamed *Moonraker* during the 1950s when Dr Peter Pye and his wife Anne crossed the Atlantic in her on a number of occasions and also cruised the Pacific. They sailed extensively for many years, wrote of their adventures and the books are now sailing classics. Now owned by Andy Pritchard of Woodbridge, Suffolk, she is presently undergoing a rebuild. These two boats are technically classed as Polperro gaffers, but they are always included with the luggers.

The *Guide Me* (FY 233), 40ft and built in Looe in 1911, was bought by Jono and Judy Brickhill and family who rebuilt her in the 1970s. They have since covered many thousands of sea miles, visiting South Africa, South America and the West Indies. A very well known boat in the sailing fraternity. Rig, dipping lug, no engine.

Guiding Star (FY 363), 40ft and built in Looe in 1907, crossed the Atlantic to Panama in the 1950s. From 1960 to 1990 she was owned by Brigadier Jack Glennie and his wife Marguerite who regularly cruised from the Baltic to Spain. She was later purchased by Barry Jobson and Jackie Gallespie who, after a major rebuild, took her on her second Atlantic crossing to the West Indies. Rig: dandy ketch.

The *White Heather* (FH 34), 38ft and built in Looe in 1926, was refitted in 2002 for an Atlantic crossing and explored the coast of Brazil and the West Indies. Rig: dandy ketch plus square foresail; skipper Mike Mckay- Lewis.

Rosalind, 45ft and built in St Ives in 1898, cruised the Mediterranean and eastern seaboard of the USA. Rig: gaff ketch; skipper Richard Griffeths.

Du Kerins (FY 290), ex-*Dos Amigos*, ex-*Our Francis*, 38ft and built in St Ives in 1920; owners Sue and Mike Darlington took a winter off to cruise in the Mediterranean, leaving and returning to their home port of Looe. Rig: dandy ketch.

Swift (FY 405), 45ft and built in Looe in 1920, became a research vessel based at the Galapagos Islands in the Pacific and was renamed *Beagle* after the brig that Charles Darwin sailed on. Sadly, she was wrecked on a reef sometime in the late 1960s. Rig: gaff ketch.

There are several others known to be voyaging about, among them are two Looe luggers, the *Janie* (FY 227) and the *Seagull* (FY 408), plus another St Ives' boat called *Gratitude*.

The luggers of Cornwall have existed in various forms for at least 400 years, fulfilling the roles of smuggler, privateer and fishing vessel. Now they are evolving again to play a new and very different role, this time as classic yachts. They are swift, sea kindly and very good-looking, causing a stir of admiration wherever they go. In particular, the harbours that the engineless ones are leaving or entering echo to the cheers and applause of onlookers as their crews bend to the sweeps. In the sailing days, regattas were held at all the major fishing ports: St. Ives, Newlyn, Mevagissey and Looe. These events were well attended, not only by the home port's fleet, but by the 'flyers' from other harbours. There was great prestige for your boat and town if you scooped the silverware at another port's regatta, as with the *Little Charlie* at Mevagissey. When engines became more reliable and powerful enough, the sailing rigs were cut right back and eventually abandoned altogether. So were the regattas, nobody saw much skill or challenge in motoring around a course, although in recent times the trawler race has become an important event at some of the bigger harbours.

The massive upsurge of interest in historic and classic sail in the latter quarter of the last century led to some of us at Looe doing some research and coming to the conclusion that there were just enough of the old boats back under sail to reinstate the regatta under the banner of the Cornish Lugger Association. So, in June 1989, a sight was seen in Looe bay that was then only remembered by some of the oldest residents: sailing luggers racing for silver cups. After a break of 78 years, they were back.

Our first event was attended by about five actual luggers, so to pack out the numbers and make it a bit more of a spectacle we invited various other classic boats from around the coast to attend as well, which they very kindly did. That weekend was hailed as a great success and, with the publicity it enjoyed, the foundations were laid for much greater things. Our regatta is now held biannually and is usually attended by 20-plus class 'A' luggers, the 30 to 45 foot fully-decked type, and as many class 'B' vessels, 18 to 25 feet, open or part-decked boats, pretty little craft that originally gained their living on the inshore fishery working crab pots, hand lines and drift nets. The nickname for these boats was 'two men on a plank'.

The biggest section of that class is made up by the Beer luggers, chunky, tough, clinker-built open boats of around 20 foot in length, once used in the sprat and crab fishery working off the open beach. Today they can still be seen hauled up to the top of that Devon beach, but now they are sailed for pleasure by a crowd of enthusiasts under the heading of the Beer Lugger Club. A lovely gang, who attend our regatta with a dozen or so boats, and by the time family and friends join in, their party alone numbers about 50 people. Our event would not be the same without them.

Vessels from Brittany voyage over to join in, adding a huge helping of laughter, music and song to the proceedings. One of them is the *Grande Lejon*, a St. Brieuc lugger that has attended all our events since she was launched in 1992. Her crew are a real fun crowd and they have made many friends in Looe over the years.

The sailing gigs also create a lot of interest. These lean, brightly-painted craft knife around the bay at a great rate, looking like large wind-assisted pencils. You have to be bright-eyed and bushy-tailed to sail one of them in a fresh breeze.

At Looe we try to maintain the spirit of the old regattas. It is, first and foremost, an event for the boats and their crews, although the weekend does boost the economy of the town a fair bit as hundreds of people come to watch the racing. Hotels, guesthouses and holiday cottages do well as vacations are booked to coincide with our event, and this has a spin off for the shops, pubs and restaurants, which is all to the good as many of our sponsors run such businesses. But unlike some festivals, the boats are not kept alongside the quay for the weekend to act as harbour dressing to attract the maximum number of visitors. After about ten o'clock, the harbour is empty and all the boats are in the bay hoisting sail in readiness for the racing; the atmosphere is electric.

Race days mean an early start for Leo Bowdler and his son Brian. For many years they have volunteered their trawler *Maret* as the committee boat, and to this end they are out in the bay long before most have even stirred out of their bunks. So, by the time the luggers leave the quay, Leo and Brian have gauged the weather, laid out the course then come to anchor to form the start line. For the rest of us, the day begins just after breakfast. By then crowds of locals and visitors are strolling the quays watching the crews as they make their boats ready for sea and head out into the bay to set sail and jockey for a good position on the starting line.

Once the starting cannon is fired on the committee boat, the luggers storm over the line heeling to the breeze with every stitch of canvas set, the skippers clinging to the tillers while the crews trim the sails to get every last ounce of speed out of them. On the press boats, the television cameras roll and photographers from the local papers snap away as if there was a prize for the one taking the most pictures. All the while a flotilla of pleasure boats weaves around the racing fleet trying to gain the best view. Ashore, hundreds of people gather on the cliffs overlooking the bay to watch this wonderful sight, binoculars and cameras at the ready. If the sun is shining and the breeze is just right, everyone seems to be brimming with happiness and the atmosphere in the town over that weekend is unique.

On the Saturday night a dance is held under the fish market with a band and bar, and once the alcohol has worked its magic, it's not just the young ones that are up strutting their stuff. Dance styles that were honed to perfection in discos many years ago are once more in evidence as fine demonstrations of wedding reception style 'Dad' dancing break out. I have even seen a few old ravers up flicking a dusty hoof with walking sticks in hand, bless 'em all.

Sunday night is prize-giving night, an event that has become rather predictable in the class 'A' section; the winners from way back are still the winners today, and do what they may, the other boats just can't touch them. First place has always been taken by the *Guide Me* (FY 233) while second and third places are shared between the 1903 Mevagissey lugger *Reliance* (FY 59) and the 1898 Porthleven-built *George Glasson* (FH 173). The sailing performance of these very ancient craft is nothing short of astounding; they cut through the rest of the fleet like a knife through butter and will very often lap them. To the more competitive crews left in their wake, they are a benchmark to try and come up to: new and bigger sails are cut, new sheet leads are tried and a multitude of modifications take place, but so far the flyers seem to be virtually untouchable. But not to worry, the Olympic games maxim, as corny as it may sound, rings very true at the Looe regatta: 'It's not the winning but the taking part that counts', but I know several skippers who would say. "Bollocks, you wait until the next time!" In truth though, it's both those attitudes that make a good classic boat regatta, and long may it be so.

Postscript

The five luggers working out of Looe when I first went to sea are all still in service. The *Guide Me* was rebuilt and re-rigged by Jono and Judy Brickhill, bringing up four children aboard while she was their home for many years. They have cruised her extensively, winning the Antigua classics in the West Indies and today she is the flyer of the fleet.

The *Our Daddy* fished from Looe until the early 1980s. She was then bought by a Plymouth businessman who had her extensively rebuilt and converted into a no-expense spared luxury classic yacht which rather gives her the air of a grand old duchess. Now owned by Looe businessman Mike Cotton in partnership with her skipper Mike Darlington, they do charter work and day sailing from Looe.

After many years in limbo, the *Eileen* is now back in good order, thanks to the hard work put in by her owner and skipper Lorain Harris of Penryn. She is a dipping lug rig and can be seen every summer taking part in the local regattas.

The *Our Boys* is splendidly refitted as a charter yacht, sporting a massive standing lug rig. She is now working out of Cowes in the Isle of Wight under skipper Richard Parr.

Last, but not least, is my old ship the *Iris*. When her fishing days ended in the early 1970s she eventually became a houseboat. Later a local shipwright, Andy Scantlebury, made her into a gaff ketch yacht. Based at Falmouth, he and his family lived on her for several years. Sold on, she suffered a couple of very indifferent owners and by 2000 was in a sorry state. She is now owned by trawler skipper and marine artist Toni Knights of Brixham and is undergoing massive restoration work from the keel up. The 'Old Black Dragon' will rise again.

I visited the *Iris* at the boat yard at Galmpton, up the river from Dartmouth. Craned out high and dry her new decks and hull planking looked fine, while down below she was stripped out from end to end awaiting her new fit out. I looked aft to where the old cabin used to be and in my mind's eye I could still see the sou'westers and mufflers swinging gently from their nails beside each bunk, the old Lister engine clattering away while the coal range puffed smoke from its open door. In his usual corner Harry sat rolling fags from a tin of dog-ends, while up top the decks were once more crowded with baskets of line, and there was 'Tiddler', Clarence, 'Moogie' and Jack.

For a brief flash of time it was like watching a piece of film that I had somehow stepped into and become part of. I could see, hear and smell it all again. Then someone spoke and the spell was broken; I was no longer 16-years-old and out lining in the Channel, I was nearer 60 and standing in a boatyard in Devon.

Glossary

AMIDSHIPS: Mid section of a vessel.

BACKSTAY: Part of a masts standing rigging.

BAR: The piece of twine that forms one side of a net mesh.

BAULKS: Large beams of timber.

BEAM: Width of a vessel across the deck at her widest point.

BELAYING: Making fast or tying off.

BENDS: Heavy oak timbers to reinforce the hull of a boat.

BIGHT: A loop of rope.

BILGE: Bottom of a boat in the mid section.

BULWARKS: The extension of the hull above the deck to stop fish, gear and crew from going overboard. On a lugger this was set at knee height.

BULKHEAD: A partition on a boat.

BUTT: Formed by two planks meeting end to end on a frame.

CABIN SOLE: Cabin floor.

CAPSTAN: Mechanical device to haul ropes and cables.

CARVEL: Planking method where planks lay edge to edge.

CAULKING: To pack seams of planks with a waterproof material to prevent leaking.

CLINKER: A method of planking a boat where the plank edges overlap.

COAMINGS: The frame around a deck opening, usually 10 or 12inches higher than the deck itself.

CRAN: A measure of fresh herrings - 37½ gallons (about 750 fish)

CRUDDY: Feeling seasick.

DANN: A bouy used to mark the end of a net, a long-line or a fleet of crab pots. A flag is fixed to it.

DEADWOOD: Baulks of oak laid between keel and sternpost and keel and stem to add strength.

DIXIE: A big stew pot.

DRAUGHT: Depth of hull from waterline to keel.

DRUDGING: To control a vessels speed by dragging astern a lump of ballast iron or chain.

FATHOM: 6 feet.

FRAMES: Inside skeleton of vessel that carry the planks, usually made of oak.

GUNNELS OR GUNWHALES: The top outside rail of a boat.

GYPSY: A gear wheel that carries the steering chain at the wheel.

JIB: Triangular sail set between mast head and bowsprit.

JOWTER: Fish seller, usually working from a van or a cart.

KEEL: Heavy elm or oak baulk, forming the backbone of a boat.

KEVEL: A stout oak bar bolted across two stanchions to make a strong point for mooring ropes.

KNOTS: Speed of a vessel through the water, based on a nautical mile of 2000 yards.

LEG: A stout baulk of timber shaped to fit the up and down shape of a boat amidships. This is to prevent a vessel going over on her side at low tide when working from a drying harbour.

MAUND BASKET: A heavy circular two handled wicker basket that held about five stone.

MIZZEN: Aft mast sail on a fore and aft rigged vessel.

PARTING BOARDS: Boards eight or ten inches in height set fore and aft on the deck to prevent the catch from sliding about.

PAWL: A ratchet device on the end of the hauling roller.

PEAK: The top most part of a sail.

POLE END BOUY: The very last buoy on a fleet of drift nets.

QUARTERS: The port and starboard aft sections of a boat.

RUDDER: Steering device at stern of boat.

SUANT: The lines of a vessel looking fair and sweet.

SHEAR LINE: The line of a boat running fore and aft at the deck or rail.

SHEET: A tackle to control a sail.

SIDEWINDERS: Trawlers that haul and shoot their gear over the side as against the modern method of over the stern (stern draggers).

SKIRT: The lower section of a drift net.

SPELL: A rest or breather.

STEM: The very front part of the bow, linking the keel to the deck and carrying the plank ends.

STERNPOST: An oak post linking keel to deck, carrying the transom or, if a double ender, the plank ends.

THREE'ERS: Two broken bars requiring three knots to repair.

TRANSOM: The flat stern of a vessel, usually made of oak.

WATERWAYS: The narrow part of the deck between the net room coamings and the rail.

YARN: To talk or tell a story.

The Author

Paul Greenwood was born in Looe in 1947. His father was a shipwright by trade, later to become a cabinet maker and antique restorer, his mother a schoolteacher. The eldest of four children, he has two sisters, Penny and Louise, and a brother, Nick. He went to sea at the age of 16, joining the *Iris* in 1964. He later sailed as bosun aboard the *Malcolm Miller* before returning to fishing in 1973 and buying his own boat, the lugger *Ibis*, in 1978 which he used until 2002. He now lives in East Looe and owns the sailing lugger *Erin*. His second book, *More Tales From A Cornish Lugger*, was published in 2011.

Acknowledgements

Photographs reproduced by kind permission of John Southern, Bill Cowan, Mike Pengelly and the author.